Getting into

Veterinary School

James Barton
8th edition

Getting into Veterinary School

This 8th edition published in 2011 by Trotman Publishing an imprint of Crimson Publishing Limited, Westminster House, Kew Road, Richmond, Surrey TW9 2ND

© Trotman Publishing 2011

Author: James Barton

7th edn by James Barton published in 2009
6th edn by Mario De Clemente published in 2007
5th edn by Mario De Clemente published in 2005
4th edn by James Burnett published in 2003
3rd edn by James Burnett published in 2001
2nd edn by John Handley published in 1999 as *Getting Into Veterinary Science*
1st edn by John Handley published in 1999 as *Getting Into Veterinary Science*

Editions 1–6 published by Trotman and Co Ltd

British Library Cataloguing in Publication Data
A catalogue record for this book is available from the British Library.

ISBN 978 1 84455 390 7

Typeset by IDSUK (DataConnection) Ltd.
Printed and bound in the UK by Ashford Colour Press, Gosport, Hants.

Getting into
Veterinary
School

Getting Into guides

Contents

Contents

About the author

James Barton has been a Director of Studies and a careers adviser at Mander Portman Woodward's London college since September 2007. As well as being the author of MPW *Getting into Physiotherapy Courses*, James has sat on interview and audition panels and given careers advice across a range of fields.

Acknowledgements

I would like to thank everybody who has contributed to the eighth edition of *Getting into Veterinary School*. I am particularly grateful to James Burnett, Maya Waterstone and my family for their advice, guidance and practical support, and for their patience in listening to my animal idioms! I am grateful to Lianne Carter and Petrouchka Stafford for their efforts. I would also like to thank Guy Beynon, Emma Godwin, Emma Lumley and Katarina Lees for allowing their UCAS personal statements to be included in the book and everyone else who contributed to the previous editions of this book. Particular thanks should go to the staff and students at the UK veterinary schools, and to both UCAS and the RCVS.

James Barton
September 2010

Introduction
'Do I have a cat in hell's chance . . .?!'

Are you running around like a headless chicken? Or are you going about this like a bull in a china shop? Well, the aim of this book is to kill as many birds as possible with one stone. After all, there is truth in the idiom that the early bird catches the worm. The last thing you want is for your application to resemble a dog's dinner or even mutton dressed as lamb, and therefore one cannot overvalue the importance of meticulous planning. So if you feel like a fish out of water and have butterflies in your stomach about the UCAS process, don't despair: this guide is here to help you cope. And remember, stay positive – every dog does have its day. The last thing we want is for you to feel as though there's an elephant sitting on your chest! Be dogged in your determination and work like a beaver. If you horse around, feathers will fly. Don't be too selective with your choices – a bird in the hand is worth two in the bush.

All right, enough animal clichés for now, but it is important that you note that while the process of applying to veterinary schools will help to shape your future career choice, you should never let it get to the stage where it grinds you down. Aside from anything else, by the end of this book, you should have an answer to the feline question above and be the one that got the cream instead of using up one of your nine lives! And so to business.

Someone once said to me, 'If you are allergic to animals, being a vet might not be the best career path.' This might sound like a ridiculous statement, but it does make a half-decent point: make sure your career decision is well thought out. In 2009, there were 1,980 applicants for entry to veterinary school. Of these, 885 were accepted, a success rate of 45%: and 105 were accepted through Clearing – however, these people most probably already held offers but narrowly missed the grades in the summer exams. For those aspiring to join the veterinary profession, the most important question is 'What can I do to make sure that I am in that 45% when I apply?' The aim of this book is to supply you with that information. However, there is no secret formula that will ensure success. The students who are accepted work hard to gain their places. They are motivated and determined, and their desire to work in the field of veterinary science is deep-rooted and genuine. Having said that, without adequate preparation, even the most promising candidate will not get a place if they do not fulfil the required criteria.

This book should in no way be seen as dissuasive. It is about getting into veterinary school – it is not designed to put you off and push you towards something else. The tone reflects a balanced mixture of realism and optimism. No one should underestimate the hard road that lies ahead. Getting into one of the seven veterinary schools in the UK (Nottingham became the seventh in 2006) is just the first stage on the route to becoming a qualified veterinary surgeon, with all the inevitable hard work and dedication that will follow in the next 40 years or so. The key to success lies within each individual.

Academic ability is not merely a requirement, it is an absolute necessity. Unless you have the clear potential to study science in the sixth form, this book alone cannot help you. Students attracted towards veterinary science should have a natural academic ability in the sciences. A confident prediction of high grades at A level is a great help, but even that will not be enough on its own to get into one of the veterinary schools. You will have to show proof of your interest, enthusiasm and commitment – you will have to show that this is what you really want.

So how do you know that this is the career for you and that you are not wasting your own and everyone else's time? If you are asking yourself this, your number one priority must be to become well enough informed about and acquainted with the work of a vet to ensure that you have made the right choice of career and to safeguard against regrets further down the line. And once you know this, what do you need to consider next?

- What are the factors involved in choosing a course? Have you considered all of them?
- What do the courses have in common?
- What are the factors that influence admissions tutors to come down in favour of one well-qualified candidate against another?
- What happens at interview?
- What about the various career choices open to the newly qualified vet?
- What do customers who use the services of a veterinary surgeon look for in a 'good' vet?
- Does this sound like the kind of profession that would suit you?

Putting academic skill to one side for a moment, would you feel comfortable dealing with your customers as well as the animals? The first thing you learn in veterinary practice is that all animals bring an owner with them. How would you handle a sceptical Dales man or an elderly lady who is anxious and watchful as you come into contact with her beloved pet? Animals play a crucial part in the lives of their owners and whether the vet handles this with tact and understanding will be the deciding factor in both their professional and their personal development. This book will help those who feel drawn to the career for sentimental reasons to understand the realities – good and bad – of being a vet and enable you to evaluate whether you have what it takes to follow this path.

A feature of this book is real students' views. Many people who are now undergraduates on veterinary courses say that they would have appreciated knowing the views of people in their position when they were at school. Panels of students returning to their former schools to give careers advice often do not include a veterinary student. This book, therefore, includes several student profiles, the first of which is given below. It also introduces you to the key features of the veterinary degree courses available, guides you through the UCAS application process, with specific reference to veterinary schools, and provides expert advice on preparing for an interview. Topical and controversial issues, any of which could come up at interview, are highlighted and career options outlined. Finally, the book includes useful contacts and sources of information to assist you with further research.

Case study

Thomas, who is 21 years old, comes from Liverpool and is now in the third year of his veterinary medicine course at the University of Liverpool. He grew up on the Wirral, and he knew that he wanted to live near home as this was where all his friends and family were. Sometimes the heart is where the home is!

Thomas's ambition to be a vet developed at an early age: 'From about the age of 14, I was on the path to being a vet. Our home was like a menagerie with three different types of exotic birds (including a parrot) and, strangely, a cat; it was like something out of *Looney Toons*! I took an avid interest in their health and well-being, which might sound peculiar, especially seeing that all my friends spent their time having a kick around. This did not concern me though, and I spent my time helping on local farms with the husbandry of the animals – cleaning the pens and feeding the cows and pigs. Off the back of this, I met a local vet who gave me an opportunity to find out more about the business in his general practice in Northwich. This was an amazing experience, even though on the first day I witnessed a lethal injection being given to a dog who had been seriously injured by a road accident. I was devastated but I quickly came to appreciate that this is part and parcel of a vet's role and those experiences have only served to harden my resolve.

'Through the UCAS process, I applied to the Royal Veterinary College London, Bristol, Cambridge and of course Liverpool. Despite living in the north all my life, Scotland was just a step too far! With a strong sense of purpose in my mind, I achieved strong GCSE and A level grades in Biology, Chemistry and Religious Studies – for a bit of variety! Knowing that I was finally about to embark on the course that would shape my future was an incredible buzz and arriving at the University of Liverpool on the first day was the proudest moment of my life to date. Three years down the line I have absolutely no regrets. I suppose I am just irritable now waiting to start my actual career!'

There's no pleasing some people.

1 | The bare necessities
What is the role of a vet?

This is perhaps the most pertinent question of all because the answer to that question must reflect the considerable sacrifice in terms of time and effort that every vet makes. Every veterinary practice has to be organised so that someone is on call 24 hours a day, for 365 days a year. As one farmer commented, 'A vet needs to have a really good sense of humour to be called out at 3 a.m. on a cold night to deal with a difficult calving and having to get down in six inches of muck!' It is certainly not a career for someone lacking in confidence, or who holds back and carries an air of uncertainty. Vets are still held in high esteem. The popular image of a vet is of someone working long hours, who is able and caring, whose charges are not too high and who doesn't worry too much about bills being paid promptly! While this closing sentiment might be ambitious, the popular view is in fact the accurate view.

James Herriot (an English veterinary surgeon and writer) would probably do these words more justice at this stage: he reveals in his books what the profession really entails. In his first book, *If Only They Could Talk*, he reflects on the unpredictability of animals and indeed a vet's life as a whole: 'It's a long tale of little triumphs and disasters,' writes Herriot, 'and you've got to really like it to stick it . . . One thing, you never get bored.' On another occasion, Herriot muses, with aching ribs and bruises all over his legs, that being a vet is, in fact, a strange way to earn a living.

> '*But then I might have been in an office with the windows tight shut against the petrol fumes and the traffic noise, the desk light shining on the columns of figures, my bowler hat hanging on the wall. Lazily I opened my eyes again and watched a cloud shadow riding over the face of the green hill across the valley. No, no . . . I wasn't complaining.*'

Some people grumble about the beguiling influence of the Herriot books. There is, however, a lot of cool reality in the pages laden with good humour and philosophy; so much so that one student described the effect of the books as leaving a 'cold afterglow'. Many professions would love to have a PR agent with the skills of Herriot writing on their behalf.

So what makes a good vet?

- Confidence
- Authority
- Composure
- Nerve
- Empathy – for both patient and client
- Versatility
- Focus
- Organisation
- Resilience
- Being well informed
- Knowing one's limitations
- Good judgement, i.e. prevention versus cure
- And, above all, a thick skin.

If you have these qualities, a career in veterinary medicine is a strong possibility. Vets are incredibly resilient people who deal with a variety of challenges on a weekly, often daily, basis. You must have confidence in your own abilities and your own judgement, but you must also have the strength to communicate effectively and authoritatively. Bear in mind that you will be calling the shots because you will be the expert.

A good vet can diagnose most things, but if they cannot, it is their job to know who can. The secret is to know your own limitations. This is particularly important for the newly qualified veterinary surgeon. 'New vets,' according to experienced Cheshire farmer David Faulkner, 'must know when to seek help and be mature enough not to be too embarrassed, for there are always a lot of new things still to learn.'

The farmer's view

'Farmers know immediately if they are going to get on with you,' an experienced vet revealed. 'They look at the way you handle and approach the animals. If you can't catch them, the owner will lose confidence and you won't be allowed anywhere near the livestock.' A seasoned farmer confided, 'Give me a vet who doesn't wait to be asked and is out giving you a hand.' He added, 'If they are confident in what they are doing it soon comes across.' Farmers and animal owners generally like to have a vet who communicates well, has a sense of humour, is outgoing rather than shy and reserved, and is able to walk into any situation and have an answer. There is a stigma about women in the profession and the capability of female vets in large animal situations. The truth of the matter is that if you choose to specialise in this field (no pun intended), gender issues will disappear if you are confident and firm.

Prevention

Even with the technological advances of the 21st century, prevention makes sense. Animals simply cannot tell you when they are unwell, so a good vet will seek to promote preventive medicine whenever possible. Today there is a lot of knowledge about preventive health by diet and vaccination. Whole herds can be treated at the right time of year. Farmers expect their vet to look ahead and draw their attention to what will prevent disease: 'Look, October is approaching – why not vaccinate all the cattle and prevent pneumonia?' If you give this kind of advice you will inspire faith in those you are seeking to help. Additives can be administered in either the feed or drink. This is much better than having to go through the trauma of having to inject a whole farmyard of pigs! A vet can do a lot of good with vaccinations and treating deficiencies through the feed by replacing what is not there, improving not only productivity but also the welfare of the animals.

Most people will agree that prevention is better than cure, but sometimes this is a naive statement to make. Preventive medicine is costly and farmers, in particular, have a reputation for being frugal. There is no doubt that preventive medicine is a good investment for the future, but in the aftermath of BSE (bovine spongiform encephalopathy), foot-and-mouth disease, and the collapse of much of their export market, farmers are anxious and, in many cases, unwilling to make the necessary outlay. Drug usage for cattle has fallen away. Often farmers do not approach the vet until there is an emergency and by then it might just be an exercise in damage limitation.

In today's busy world, with a general shortage of vets, it is not easy always to respond to this situation. It is said in the profession that you should try to take time to stop and let your eyes range over the flock or herd, looking for the one or two animals who do not fit into the general pattern and who seem out of sorts. There is also a lot to be said for encouraging good husbandry by advising on the housing of the animals. While the sign of a good vet is that he/she will have the latest drug information at their fingertips and knowledge of how to treat certain conditions, sound, informed and diplomatic advice will often earn the vet similar respect and kudos among their clients: 'Instead of me treating the animals' feet, why don't you improve that footpath?'

Small animals

Working with household animals can require a different approach. It is as much about counselling the owners as treating the patients and for that reason, interpersonal skills are a prerequisite. With pets, there is great variety – one moment you might be treating a reptile with a nutritional problem; the next, a cat losing weight might be brought in for tests and cause you to wonder if there might be a problem with its liver – or could it be cancer? A rabbit could be brought in – many are now regarded as house pets – and your initial diagnosis of myxomatosis might be confirmed. Or it could be something as mundane as placing a microchip in an animal for security purposes. Dental problems among the small-animal population occur quite frequently but obesity is also much more common than most people imagine. The vet has to advise and persuade the owner – however obstinate they might be – to reduce the animal's feed and bring it in for of regular weigh-ins at the surgery.

A lot of animals are kept in busy urban environments, thus increasing the risk of pets being involved in road accidents. If a dog that has been hit by a vehicle is brought in, the 'crash kit' may have to be used. The doses of the most commonly used drugs are marked clearly on the crash box lid, the syringes are loaded, everything is sterilised and ready. It is important to act quickly, but the true professional keeps calm; it is no time for the vet to fumble when decisive action can save the dog's life.

Arguably the most important quality required for this job is having a thick skin, especially in cases where an animal has to be euthanised. The ethical issues that affect our medical profession and the moral question of 'playing God' do not exist in the veterinary counterpart because it is often kinder to make these decisions for the good of the animal. You have to weigh up their suffering against the owner's protestations and grief and your own conscience. A good vet must find that little bit extra inside themselves. It is crucial to deal with the owners in a compassion-ate yet effective way. It has often been said that the hope and trust of the owners is matched only by the trust and helplessness of the animals. Imagine dealing with a distraught child when he's told that his pet hamster must be put down. How do you show empathy amid the boy's flood of tears? How do you discuss it with him? Perhaps the boy's parents will let you attempt to explain how the hamster feels and that soon the small animal's pain will cease and the end itself will not be felt. Even when you know it is the kindest thing to do, giving a lethal injection is still one of the toughest parts of the job.

So why do you want to be a vet?

It's important to ask yourself this because if you become a vet you will be embarking on a career without riches or glamour. Perhaps for you it is about adapting and fitting into a way of life. Is this what keeps everyone focused during the long hours of study? An interest in and sympathy for animals is taken for granted by many commentators, but in reality it is the way you react to an emergency that puts your dedication to the test. It is all in a day's (or night's) work for a vet and there is no one to applaud you except the grateful, or perhaps less understanding, owner. In short, commitment is the key, particularly if, or perhaps that should be when, the going gets tough. As a vet you must feel that you want to help, cure and take care of animals to the best of your ability whatever the weather and whatever the circumstances. It is the kind of commitment which will almost certainly have begun at a very early age and will have become stronger and more focused in your teenage and college years. Of course, while the vast majority of qualified vets are in general practice, this is not the only option open to you: you might equally choose to go into teaching, inspection or research. Yet no matter which option you pursue, the level of knowledge and commitment required is very high.

Case study

Alfie gained his A levels in 2010 and is now studying veterinary medicine at Edinburgh University. Alfie grew up in Surrey, in the countryside, and wanted to be a vet from an early age. With persistence, Alfie was able to get work experience in a small local veterinary surgery where, sadly, he had taken his dog Sam to be put down. This strengthened Alfie's resolve, though, and he wanted to help prevent other animals suffering with terminal illnesses. 'Seeing Sam die of stomach cancer was hard but it made me 100% sure that I wanted to help other animals not go through pain.'

Alfie changed school between his GCSEs and his AS level year and this helped him focus him on the academic requirements necessary to get to university. He achieved four A grades and after having two interviews at two different places, Alfie received an offer from both universities. 'What is important is that you are interested in your A level studies. If you are not then you will not get good grades. Equally, it might imply that a career in veterinary science is not for you.'

Alfie's work experience involved doing whatever work he could do alongside the vet, anything from manual labour to shearing sheep. This gave him the opportunity to ask any number of questions to help him understand the veterinary profession from the point of view of the different people who come into contact with the profession.

Alfie has enjoyed the first year of his studies, but finds some of the work hard. 'The pace is different from A level, and it is not just a question of learning notes – they want to find out if we understand as well: not like school! Another thing that makes it harder is that my parents are not around to tell me to do my homework every night, and there are lots of opportunities to go out and enjoy life. Still, I think I am just about coping but I know that I'll have to work harder next term.'

2 | Separating the sheep from the goats
Preparation and experience

Wanting to become a veterinary surgeon is a long-term commitment. It requires perseverance and a lot of determination. If all goes well and you get the kind of sixth-form science results demanded by all the veterinary schools, it will still take a further five or six years to qualify. Most people faced with the need for intensive study in the sixth form will find it hard to look further ahead than the next test or practical. Yet much more than this is needed if you are to stand a chance of getting into veterinary school.

Starting early

Ideally, the pursuit of your interest in animals and their welfare, in short, your commitment, should have started much earlier than sixth form. There are numerous cases of aspiring vets who have begun their enquiries as early as the age of 12, and certainly many have started gaining their practical experience by the age of 14.

Some vets grew up on a farm and knew that they wanted this kind of life. Others come from an urban background and have developed an interest despite not being brought up in an animal-friendly environment. This interest can be kick-started in a variety of ways and can develop through, for instance, pet ownership, the Herriot books, one of the numerous television programmes such as *Animal Park, Super Vets* and *Vet Safari*, or the influence of a friend. 'It's a great life, there's so much variety,' was one student's view. 'You realise it when you start going out getting experience. You see that you can be a vet in a town or in the countryside, that some practices are much larger than others and that some are very busy while others appear more relaxed.'

One young vet said that she had begun her enquiries at about the age of 14 and started working at weekends – her experience began with work in a stables where she began to learn horse riding. Another recalled how she had done kennel work at weekends for four years before becoming a veterinary student. It goes without saying that cleaning out kennels is a dirty, often unpleasant job, but to do this over such a long period shows an impressive degree of commitment and dedication from an early age. Some students have the chance to gain early experience on a nearby farm. But what would you do there? One farmer's wife commented, 'We would expect a 14-year-old to help feed the livestock, to help with bedding-up, which means putting fresh straw in the pens, and sweeping up.' You should be alert to what is happening around you. Before long you may start asking questions: 'Why is that calf coughing? What are you giving it?'

Getting more experience

As those pre-A level years unfold, it makes sound sense to follow up your visits to the local stables, kennels or farm with a week or two spent with your local vet. The point is that you are not just trying to find ways to satisfy the admissions tutor at veterinary school who may one day read an application that you have completed, important though that is; you are also testing your own motivation. This is vital because, make no mistake, you are going to need all the focus you can muster. The task you are about to set yourself is going to draw upon all your commitment, dedication and determination.

It should be pointed out that a student who is still at school or sixth-form college will be very lucky to find themselves in the consulting room with the vet. This is because anxious owners will not always appreciate or understand the need for someone of school age to be present. It is much more likely that you will be asked to spend time with the veterinary nurses. As one vet commented, 'Let's see if they can handle animals. Are they frightened?' The idea is to see how the student reacts to aspects of animal husbandry at an early stage. If you cannot abide cleaning up the blood and faeces that go with animal practice then you should in all probability think of another career. After an artery has stopped pumping or diarrhoea has ended, there is a clean-up job to be done and that is an early experience for many well-intentioned potential vets. Can you take it?

Confirmation of a period spent at a veterinary establishment is one of the conditions for entry to an undergraduate course leading to the degree of Bachelor of Veterinary Medicine or Science. Without getting out and finding out what it is like to deal with sick animals as well as normal, healthy ones, how will you know that you are suited to a career dedicated to providing a service to animals and their owners? As one student put it, 'Knowing what animals look like doesn't necessarily prepare you for what they feel or smell like. There is only one way to find out and that is to get into close contact.' You may think you love animals because of the way you feel about your own pet, but going from the particular to the general may cause you to think quite differently. You might even be allergic to some animals. Make certain that you still feel happy about dealing with animals in general and that you really mean business.

Specific university requirements

Work experience is also vital if you are to have a chance of being called for interview, and without an interview you cannot be offered a place. Some of the veterinary schools are more specific than others about what they expect in the way of practical experience.

- The Royal Veterinary College specifies 'at least six weeks "hands on" experience: two weeks with one or more veterinary practices; two weeks or more working with larger domestic animals on a livestock farm; and two weeks of other animal experience (e.g. kennels, riding school, zoo, etc.).'
- Cambridge is more relaxed about work experience. The Cambridge website states that 'it is helpful to have some personal experience of the veterinary profession and have a realistic idea about what the work may entail. However, extensive experience is not a prerequisite and seeing a variety of different aspects of the profession for relatively short periods can be more helpful.'
- Bristol, while stating that you must show evidence of work experience to justify an interest in the subject, gives no specific details and therefore it is left up to the applicant to acquire as much practical experience as possible prior to interview.
- Edinburgh expects applicants to have obtained practical experience in the handling and husbandry of major species, and also to have spent some time observing veterinary practice involving small animals, farm animals and horses to obtain a broad range of experience. They go on to say that work experience in a veterinary or biomedical laboratory is also useful.
- Glasgow advises applicants that 'experience working with veterinarians, so that the applicant has some understanding of the duties and responsibilities of a practitioner, is essential before making such a career choice'.
- Liverpool requires at least four weeks' experience of veterinary practice, preferably spent in more than one practice, and a further six weeks of other animal experience including farm work, stables, kennels, etc. Zoo work and visiting abattoirs can be used as work experience but they are not essential. However, experience of UK farming practices is a prerequisite.
- Nottingham is fairly open-ended and requires at least six weeks animal-related work experience and that could be in general practice, on a farm or at a stables, for example.

Making the initial contact

Making the first contact can be quite difficult, often because of your nerves, inexperience or because the vet is cautious and reluctant to take on an unknown commitment. This is where parents can help, particularly when you are pre-sixth form. If a parent knows that their son or daughter is serious and is showing promise in the sciences at school, they can be a real help by speaking to the vet and giving reassurance. Generally vets will react favourably to a parent's call because it means that the contact is serious. Once the initial approach has been made, the next stage – developing contacts – is best left to you as part of your growing self-reliance.

Your local vet will know a lot of people through working with animals. A recommendation, or better still an introduction by your local vet to a large-animal practice or a local farmer, may lead to work in a stables or work with sheep, for example. You will get to know people yourself and this will build your confidence.

Developing contacts in this way is known as networking. Taking the initiative like this can do you more favours than always relying on the careers department at your school. However, it is worth checking to see whether your school careers department can help you. Frankly, some school careers departments are much better organised than others. If the careers programme is well organised and planned on an established contact basis it would be sensible to enlist the department's help. However, do bear in mind that there is concern among some vets that placements organised by schools are not always carefully matched. If you have any doubts on this score, you will be well advised to take the initiative in making your own arrangements. Remember that in the end it is your own responsibility to get practical experience. Busy people like vets and farmers are likely to be more impressed with those who exhibit the confidence and self-reliance to make their own approaches.

What the vet will want

Some vets are reluctant to allow young, inexperienced people into their practice. This is understandable. They know that many people are attracted by the idea of becoming a vet; these people have, after all, seen many television programmes! Look at it from the vet's point of view. Some people are attracted to animals for emotional reasons; some may not be academically strong enough to make the grade; some may be so impractical that they could get their finger nipped through one of the animal cages in the first half hour. Do not be surprised if some vets suggest that you should first visit for just a day. The reason for this is that they feel they need to meet you first before committing themselves. As one vet said, 'You can get a fair idea in the first few hours; some are bright and a pleasure to have around.'

What will the local vet ask you to do? This will depend upon the vet. 'We cannot afford to waste time so we begin by asking about their capability for science A levels at grades A*, A and B,' remarked one vet. 'We give them three days of blood and gore to see what it is all about. In our case, they will see a farm. We insist on wellies and a good standard of dress, no jeans or open-necked shirts!' Alternatively, your local vet may be a small practice dealing mainly with companion animals – most often cats and dogs, but also rabbits, goldfish, gerbils and budgies. Some students may themselves have gained experience breeding bantams, ferrets, pigeons or fish. This all points to a strong interest.

Some practices are mixed, dealing with farm animals, horses and pets, while in country areas there are practices that deal mainly with farm animals. The types of practice and their size vary widely. The average practice has three or four vets: however, at the one extreme about 2% have more than 10, each with a degree of specialisation, and at the other end of the scale, about 25% are single-handed practices, requiring practitioners to deal with a wide range of work. This being so, the resources that the vet will be able to draw upon will also vary widely.

Shaping up in the surgery

A head nurse in a medium-sized mixed practice uses the following list of questions to enable her or him to judge how students helping in the small-animal surgery are shaping up. They are all well worth considering.

- How keen are they to help in every area? For example, do they clean up willingly?
- How observant are they? Do they watch how we do the bandaging or how we hold the animal straight ready for an injection? Do they watch carefully how we take a blood sample, administer an anaesthetic or set up an intravenous drip?
- Do they maintain a neat and tidy appearance and clean themselves before going in to see a small-animal client? This is very important to the owner.
- Are they friendly towards the client? Do they make conversation and try to establish a relationship?
- Do they ask questions about what they do not understand? They shouldn't be afraid to ask even while procedures are being carried out.
- Are they listening to what is being said and the way it is being said? Do they appreciate the experience that allows the vet to counsel owners on sensitive issues, for example, on reducing their favourite pet's diet? This is not an easy message to get across to an over-indulgent owner

and a vet needs a good 'bedside manner' to be able to tell the owner what must be done without giving offence.

Checklist of experience

Always take up any opportunities that you are offered. Variety of experience will not only broaden your understanding of the profession you seek to join, but will also impress the admissions tutors when they come to scrutinise your UCAS application. Here are some suggestions. Remember, some applicants to veterinary school will have carried out a few of these suggestions four or five years before applying! Others are only applicable to Year 11 or sixth-form students. But if you can tick every box by the time you submit your form in October of your upper-sixth year, well done!

- Get work experience in catteries and/or boarding kennels.
- Work in the local pet shop.
- Make contact with a local vet and indicate your interest by helping with some of the menial tasks. If you are keen you will not mind doing the dirty work.
- Get at least two to three weeks' experience with a large-animal veterinary practice or occasional days or weekends over a long period. Without this, you will not be taken into veterinary school, no matter how well qualified you are academically. You must also gain some experience of working in a companion animal practice. Some candidates are fortunate in having access to mixed practices in which they can gain familiarity with handling large and small animals.
- Visit a local dairy farm and get acquainted with farm work, which accounts for at least 30% of all veterinary science work. Try also to assist on a sheep farm at lambing time.
- Work with horses at a riding stables. (Remember that riding establishments are subject to inspection by an authorised veterinary surgeon.)
- Visit an abattoir if possible.
- Get in touch with one of the animal charities, such as the People's Dispensary for Sick Animals (PDSA) or the Royal Society for the Prevention of Cruelty to Animals (RSPCA), and find out about their work.
- Spend a day in a pharmaceutical laboratory concerned with the drugs used by vets as well as medics or a laboratory of the Department for Environment, Food and Rural Affairs (Defra).
- Try for any additional relevant experience that may be within your reach, e.g. at a zoo, where you could work as an assistant to a keeper, or in a safari or wildlife park.
- Make a point of visiting local racecourses and greyhound tracks, paying particular attention to how the animals are treated. Perhaps

your local vet has a part-time appointment to treat the horses or dogs. If the offer comes to visit with the vet you should take it.

- Visit country events such as point-to-point races, even if it is only to see what goes on. One day you may get an admissions interview and the more you know about what happens to animals in different situations the better.

Case study

Tamara studied for her A levels at an independent school in London. Her interest in veterinary science started when she was allowed to spend a day with a vet at the zoo in Battersea Park when she was 16. Organising work experience was difficult as she had school commitments on Saturdays, as well as most evenings. The veterinary practices and animal welfare organisations that she contacted wanted volunteers to work on a regular basis, and she was unable to do so. As the work experience was essential, Tamara looked for other opportunities. 'I managed to arrange work experience on a small farm in Whitechapel. Although this was hard work, it meant that I could have contact with a local vet, who visited the farm on sporadic occasions. Through him, I was able to gain more work experience, on a farm in Dorset, and this led to my being able to spend a month on a nature reserve in the summer holidays.

'I had never regarded myself as being what you might call pushy, but I found that if I demonstrated my enthusiasm, and asked for help with a smile on my face, people were only too glad to help me. I realised that I had to try to use contacts that I had made to gain work experience if I was to succeed in convincing the veterinary schools that I was serious. Of course, the point of my work experience was not only to persuade the selectors but, more importantly, to prove to myself that I really wanted to be a vet.'

Tamara sat A levels in Chemistry, Biology and Mathematics, gained A*AA, and is now studying veterinary science in Glasgow.

Variety and staying power

It is crucially important to demonstrate variety in your practical experience with animals. A visit of just one day to a veterinary practice where you watched small-animal work, followed by another visit to a mixed practice where you were able to see a surgical procedure carried out will be impressive, particularly if you can combine this with work at a stables, some contact with local farms and at least some experience in, for instance, a kennels.

But your application to veterinary school will be enhanced even further if, in addition to this, you can demonstrate a convincing commitment to one or two of the local professionals. What will impress people is the fact that you have willingly returned to your local vet's practice over a period of time and only the vet will know what it has cost you to do this. True, you will have seen a lot of interesting and varied activities and met many interesting people, but the truth is that many of your friends would have melted away had they been asked and expected to do what you have had to do. Let's face it, not many students would have returned to the practice after having to clean up and deal with blood and muck time and again.

If you can demonstrate both a variety of experience and a committed staying power, there is no doubt that this will count strongly in your favour when the competition for places in veterinary school is at its fiercest.

3 | Horses for courses
The courses

Given the competitive nature of entry into veterinary school, the idea that there is an element of choice may seem strange. Even when a candidate is fortunate enough to get two or three offers, and has to express a preference, the eventual decision is often based on things such as family connections, the recommendation of the local vet or whether or not the candidate liked the school or its locality on the open day.

Maybe decisions should be based on more objective data than this, but they seldom are. This may not be a bad thing as decisions made this way often work out quite well. However, although the courses are not vastly different, it is surely sensible for the candidate to be aware of the typical course structure and what is involved. This could be useful at interview. Most importantly, a knowledge of some of the differences between courses could play a part in your decision should you get two or more offers.

All the courses leading to a degree in veterinary science have to comply with the requirements of the Royal College of Veterinary Surgeons for recognition under the Veterinary Surgeons Act 1966. This is necessary if the degree is to gain the holder admission to the register, which confers the legal right to practise veterinary surgery. It follows that the courses are fundamentally similar; most of the slight differences come towards the clinical end of the degree. This is quite a contrast to many other degrees where the differences can be much more marked.

Veterinary courses have a carefully structured and integrated programme with one stage leading logically into the next. This logic is not always apparent to the student who may feel surprised at the amount of theoretical work in the early pre-clinical stage. Later, as you get into the para-clinical and clinical stages, it all begins to make sense. As one final year student commented, 'It's not until the fourth or fifth year that you suddenly realise "So that's why we did that!"'

The pre-clinical stage

The first two years are pre-clinical and include a lot of lectures, practicals and tutorials. The normal healthy animal is studied. A basic knowledge of the structure and function of the animal body is essential to an understanding of both health and disease. The scientific foundations are being laid with an integrated study of anatomy and physiology. This study of veterinary biological science is augmented by biochemistry, genetics and animal breeding, as well as some aspects of animal husbandry.

Veterinary anatomy

This deals with the structure of the bodies of animals. It includes: the anatomy of locomotion; cellular structure; the development of the body from egg to newborn animal; the study of body tissues such as muscle and bone; and the study of whole organs and systems such as the respiratory and digestive systems. Studying this subject involves anatomical examination of live animals with due emphasis on functional and clinical anatomy. Students spend a lot of their time examining the macroscopic and microscopic structures of the body and its tissue components. One student said, 'We seemed to look through microscopes for hours at various organs and tissues. At the time it was not easy to see the relevance, but later what we had been doing began to make a lot of sense.' There is not only detailed microscopic study of histological sections but also the study of electron micrographs of the cells that make up the different tissues.

Veterinary physiology and biochemistry

This examines how the organs of an animal's body work and their relationship to each other. This is an integral part of the first two years of the course. It is concerned with how the body's control systems work, e.g. temperature regulation, body fluids, and the nervous and cardiovascular systems. You can expect that your studies will include respiration, energy metabolism, renal and alimentary physiology, endocrinology and reproduction.

Animal husbandry

This extends throughout most courses and introduces the student to various farm livestock and related aspects of animal industries. The kind of performance expected from the different species and their respective reproductive capacities is investigated. Livestock nutrition and housing are studied, together with breeding and management. Students learn about the husbandry of domestic animals and some exotic species. Animal husbandry also involves animal handling techniques. These are important skills for the future veterinary surgeon since the patients will often be less co-operative than those met by their medical counterparts. They may even be much more aggressive than humans!

The para-clinical stage

This is sometimes referred to as the second stage. It follows on from the first two years in which normal, healthy animals are studied. Now it is time to undertake studies of disease, the various hereditary and environmental factors responsible, and its treatment. The third year usually sees the study of veterinary pathology introduced (although it sometimes begins in the second year) with parasitology and pharmacology.

Veterinary pathology

This is the scientific study of the causes and nature of various disease processes. This subject is concerned with understanding the structural and functional changes that occur in cells, tissues and organs when there is disease present.

Veterinary parasitology and microbiology

This deals with the multi-cellular organisms, small and large, which cause diseases and with bacteria, fungi and viruses. All the basic aspects of parasites of veterinary importance are studied. Students also take courses in applied immunology (the body's natural defences).

Veterinary pharmacology

This is the study of the changes produced in animals by drugs (artificial defences against disease). It comprises several different disciplines including: pharmacodynamics (the study of the mechanism of the action of drugs and how they affect the body); pharmacokinetics (absorption, distribution, metabolism and excretion of drugs) and therapeutics (the use of drugs in the prevention and treatment of disease). Some schools introduce this subject in the fourth year.

The clinical or final stage

The last two years of study build on the earlier years, with food hygiene being introduced while the study of pharmacology is deepened. The meaning of the phrase 'integrated course' now becomes apparent as all the disciplines come together. Medicine, surgery and the diseases of reproduction are taught by clinical specialists in the final stages of the course, and this part of the course is largely practical. More time is spent at the school's veterinary field station. In some cases you can expect to live in at the field station in your final year. Much of the study will be in small groups.

You will be allowed to pursue particular interests; however, the main focus will be on the prevention, diagnosis and treatment, by medical or surgical means, of disease and injury in a wide range of species.

Some practical skills learned in the clinical stage

There are many important practical skills that students have to learn in the final clinical period. One of these is the ability to examine the contents of the abdomen through the wall of the rectum without harming or causing infection to the animal through carelessness. You might also learn to use an ultrasound probe to examine, for example, the ovaries. Another use of ultrasound is to listen to the blood flow and the foetal heart sounds in a pregnant sow. Ultrasound can also assist in carrying out an examination of a horse's fetlock.

Students, like the vets they hope to become, can be called out in the middle of the night to a difficult calving. If a cow cannot give birth naturally, the student can help with a Caesarean operation. Using a local anaesthetic allows the operation to take place with the cow standing, which makes the process easier to manage. Practical skill is important with foaling. It is best if foaling takes place quickly because it is less stressful for the foal, and students are taught that all that is needed is a gentle but firm pull. Final-year students can assist with lambing, even the birth of twin lambs. There are many other examples, too numerous to mention.

The use of general anaesthetic can extend from a full range of horse treatments to vasectomising a ram. Many other techniques are also taught: for example, students might look at images of the nasal passages of a horse and see the nasal discharge from a guttural pouch infection. Another example is learning the right way to trim a cow's foot. All animals (that have them!) can suffer problems with their legs or feet. The experienced veterinary surgeon has to have the skill and confidence to be able to remove a cyst from a sheep's brain without causing a rupture.

No wonder, then, that at this final clinical stage students find that all the earlier preparation comes together and makes sense as clinical problem after problem requires you to think and reason from basic scientific principles. Examples such as these do convey the varied nature of the veterinary surgeon's work, but it is as well to remember that in addition to the physician side of the job there is a lot of routine 'dirty' work. Students have, for example, to help maintain cleanliness in the stables and enclosures of the field station. In due course, when you become a working vet, you may at some stage have to tramp round a muddy farmyard on a cold wet day carrying out blood tests on hundreds of cattle.

Remember that this summary of some of the clinical work encountered on the courses is far from comprehensive and should not lead students to believe that this corresponds to a job description.

Extramural rotation (EMR)

This is sometimes called 'seeing practice' and the time is divided between farming work and experience in veterinary practice. Students are required during the first two years to complete 10–12 weeks of livestock husbandry, depending on which school they attend. Students usually arrange this experience themselves during their vacations, and on the whole they do not seem to have too much difficulty finding a place.

Veterinary schools have lists of contacts in their own area whom you can get in touch with. A modest amount of pay can be arranged directly with the farmer. During the third, fourth and final clinical years students must complete approximately 26 weeks of seeing practice. This will be mainly with veterinary surgeons in mixed general practice, with much shorter periods in, for example, laboratory diagnostic procedures and one or two weeks in an abattoir. Casebooks have to be kept and presented at the final examination.

Notes on the courses

Bristol

Students are based in Bristol for the first three years of the course, and at Langford for the last two. Some units in Years 1, 2 and 3 are taught by pre-clinical departments which are also responsible for teaching science, medical and dental students. This encourages cross-fertilisation of ideas and access to the latest research findings in other scientific fields.

Assessment: Mainly by examination, normally in January and June each year, although there is also some assessed coursework.

Re-sits: There is usually a chance to re-sit all or part of the examination in September if the required standard is not reached in June.

Intercalation: Students may interrupt their studies for a year at the end of the second or third year in order to gain additional training for a BSc degree in, for example, Biochemistry, Microbiology, Pathology, Pharmacology or Zoology.

Clinical training: The clinical part of the Veterinary School is at Langford in the Mendip Hills, about 13 miles out of Bristol. The site hosts a wide range of small-animal, equine and farm facilities including first-opinion practices and referral hospitals. There is also a veterinary laboratories agency and abattoir on site. Students may be placed with leading local practices and farms during their lecture-free final year. The emphasis is very much on small-group clinical rotations.

Cambridge

This is the smallest of the veterinary schools. The course extends for six years and is divided equally between the pre-clinical and clinical parts.

The first two years are concerned with the basic medical and veterinary sciences, between which there is much common ground at this early stage, bringing you into contact with students from other disciplines. There are also more applied courses in farm animal husbandry and preparing for the veterinary profession. For the third year, you can elect to study in depth a subject of your own choice from a wide range of options, leading to the award of the BA (Hons) degree at the end of Year 3. The flexibility of the tripos system is one of its most attractive features.

Clinical training: The clinical training course is taught in the Department of Veterinary Medicine at the West Cambridge Campus on Madingley Road. The emphasis is on small-group practical teaching. The final year is lecture-free with hands-on experience and a period of elective study. The Farm Animal Practice provides first-opinion clinical services to surrounding farms, including the University Dairy Farm just a few miles away. A Farm Animal Referral Centre was opened in 2002. Advantage is also taken of the nearby RSPCA clinic, specialist equine practices in and around Newmarket and the Animal Health Trust Centre. There are facilities for equine work and there is also a small-animal surgical suite. Opportunities for research ensure that veterinary teaching is embedded in the latest, cutting-edge discoveries.

Edinburgh

Long established and one of the larger veterinary schools, the Royal (Dick) School of Veterinary Studies can trace its origins back to 1823. It was the first veterinary school to be established in Scotland and the second in the UK. The school is now part of the College of Medicine and Veterinary Medicine, and traditional boundaries between subjects have been reduced. Most of the pre-clinical training is at Summerhall, close to the city centre. Formal teaching is completed in four years, with the final year devoted to clinical experience.

Assessment: Half of the assessment is continuous, with the balance by examination and practicals.

Re-sits: There is a chance to re-sit the examinations in August if the required standard is not met in June.

Intercalation: Students may interrupt their studies at the end of Year 2, 3 or 5 to take a BSc (VetSc) degree in Biochemistry, Neuroscience, Microbiology and Infection or Pre-clinical Sciences. Also available is a one-year MSc by research after the third year of studies and students may do an intercalated three-year PhD during the course of studies.

Clinical training: Takes place at the Easter Bush Veterinary Centre, six miles south of the city. The centre houses the college farm, which is attached to the university's School of Agriculture, the Large Animal Practice, Equine and Food Animal Hospitals and the new Small Animal Hospital. The Centre for Tropical Veterinary Medicine forms part of the school. The Biotechnology and Biological Sciences Research Council's (BBSRC) Moredun Research Institute, the Roslin Institute and a veterinary investigation centre are situated nearby.

Glasgow

Founded in 1862, this is one of the larger schools. It has the unique advantage of being situated on a single site at Garscube, four miles to the north-west of Glasgow. On the site are the pre-clinical and clinical departments, as well as the Weipers Centre for Equine Welfare, a small-animal hospital, and nearby is Cochno Farm and Research Centre, which is used by the university as an additional teaching facility. Some pre-clinical teaching is conducted at the main university campus near the city centre, which enables students to benefit from the opportunities at both sites. The faculty is one of only four veterinary schools in Europe to be accredited to British, European and American standards.

Re-sits: These can take place in September of each year. A second failure may result in repeating a year; normally this is only possible for one year of the course.

Intercalation: At the end of Year 3, students may study for a one-year BSc (VetSc) Honours degree before starting the clinical training. Eight subjects are available. A two-year intercalated BSc Honours degree at the end of either Year 2 or Year 3 is another possibility.

Clinical training: The lecture-free final year maximises the opportunities for small-group clinical teaching around live animal cases. This takes place at the faculty's busy referral hospital and through extramural study undertaken in practices and other veterinary institutions in the UK and overseas.

Liverpool

This was the first veterinary school to be incorporated into a university structure and therefore the first to establish a university-certified veterinary degree. The Faculty of Veterinary Science celebrated its centenary in 2004. There are two degree courses leading to BVSc MRCVS: the D100, which is a five-year course; and the D101, which is a six-year course incorporating an intercalated BSc. The options for intercalating include a BSc in Conservation Medicine and an MSc in Veterinary Infectious Disease and Control. These courses are also offered to students from other veterinary schools. In 2001, the faculty also introduced a three-year BSc (Hons) course in Bioveterinary Science. Teaching on this course is shared between the Faculty of Veterinary Science and the School of Biological Sciences. Veterinary students spend the first three years of the course on campus in Liverpool studying pre-clinical and para-clinical subjects. The course is modularised. During the fourth and final years, the students are based at Leahurst, the teaching hospital on the Wirral Peninsula 18 miles away, which has facilities for equine and livestock cases and a small-animal hospital. First-opinion work (dealing with calls from clients) is undertaken at Fern Grove practice in Liverpool. There are two separate practices operating out of Leahurst, serving the large local equine population and the agricultural sector, which also get referrals from all over northern England for horses with colic, skin tumour and orthopaedic conditions. Farm visits and investigations extend to the sheep farming areas of north Wales and the dairy farms of Cheshire and Lancashire. Leahurst is in close proximity to Chester Zoo and there is a strong interest in wildlife diseases and animal behaviour.

London

The Royal Veterinary College (RVC), based in Camden Town, is the oldest and largest of the seven UK veterinary schools and one of only two veterinary schools in England accredited by both European and US authorities. As one of the University of London's 19 self-governing colleges, the RVC is the UK's only independent veterinary school and it also has a Centre for Excellence in Teaching and Learning. The RVC has developed innovative approaches to learning, and students are equipped with the knowledge and skills needed to succeed throughout their working life. Students spend their first two years undertaking comprehensive pre-clinical studies at the Camden Campus, and then proceed to clinical studies at the Hawkshead Campus in Hertfordshire (north of London).

Intercalation: Students may intercalate a BSc after successful completion of, normally, the second year. Students can also be considered for certain BSc courses offered by University of London colleges or other universities, or for the RVC's own veterinary pathology course.

Clinical training: In Year 3, students begin their clinical extramural studies at a variety of veterinary placements, eventually totalling 26 weeks (up to six of these weeks can be overseas) by the middle of Year 4. Most of the remaining time will then be spent gaining hands-on experience in RVC clinics and hospitals (intramural rotations). During Year 4, students will also spend at least eight weeks devising and executing a research project on any aspect of veterinary science that interests them.

Nottingham

Based at the university's Sutton Bonington Campus, Nottingham's School of Veterinary Medicine and Science accepted its first students in 2006. It aims to equip students with all the necessary diagnostic, medical and surgical skills. Its course integrates clinical medicine and surgery with pathology and basic sciences, to ensure that its graduates gain the best possible foundations for a career in the veterinary profession. Studies will include time spent at the new purpose-built clinical teaching facilities and at local clinical practitioners. The five-year degree course leads students from day one through a clinically integrated curriculum providing learning in all aspects of veterinary medicine and surgery. In Years 1 and 2, students undertake a minimum of 12 weeks' animal husbandry extramural studies and at least four weeks of clinical extramural studies in Year 2. All students undertake a research project in Year 3, and a minimum of 12 weeks of clinical extramural studies in both Year 3 and Year 4. At the end of Year 3, students graduate with a Bachelor of Veterinary Medical Sciences. The summer term of Year 4 and the whole final year is spent in clinical rotations. This includes a minimum of 10 weeks' extramural studies. Another 25 weeks of intramural rotations are undertaken in Year 5. Intramural rotations may include time at both large and small-animal practices, laboratory facilities and specialist facilities. After five years of successful study the degrees of Bachelor of Veterinary Medicine and Bachelor of Veterinary Surgery are awarded.

Table 1 Typical student offers 2010/11

University	A levels required	A levels preferred	Preferred grades	Access course available	Subjects required	BTEC accepted	Widening participation policy
Bristol	2	3	AAB+BMAT	No	Biology and Chemistry	Yes	Yes
Cambridge	3	3	A*AA+BMAT	No	Biology or Chemistry or Physics or Maths	N/A	Yes
Edinburgh	3	3	AAB	No	Chemistry (A) and Biology or either Physics or Maths	No	Yes
Glasgow	3	3	AAB	No	Chemistry (A) and Biology or either Physics or Maths	No	Yes
Liverpool	3.5	3.5	AABb	No	Biology and other sciences	Yes	Yes
Nottingham	3	3	AAB+AAB (Vet Med + Prelim Yr)	Certificate in Health Sciences at Lincoln University	Chemistry and Biology and a third subject	N/A	Yes
Royal Veterinary College	3	3	AAA+BMAT	Veterinary Gateway course	Chemistry and Biology and a third subject	N/A	Yes

4 | Counting sheep
Financing your course

Once you arrive in veterinary school you will want at least to avoid the worry of getting too deeply into debt. Money is a problem for all students and those studying veterinary science will have additional expenses connected with their course, mainly travel expenses, clothing, books and equipment. Veterinary students are also limited in the opportunities they have to earn extra money during vacations because they have to spend time doing extramural rotations to gain the prescribed experience in veterinary practice as part of their training. Students believe that sixth-formers and others preparing to go to veterinary school should be forewarned about coping with the money side of being a veterinary student.

First-year expenditure for veterinary students is particularly high and can easily exceed £8,000 for those living away from home.

Keeping costs down: hints and tips

- Avoid buying lots of kit or textbooks in advance. When you get to the course you may find some discounts are offered. Second-hand textbooks may be for sale, although many veterinary students prefer to keep their textbooks for use in their working lives. Also try medical students for second-hand textbooks.
- Check for student travel concessions; get advice on the best offers on the regular trips that you will have to make.
- Apply early for the student loan, as it takes some time for the loan to be processed. Remind the bank about that overdraft facility they promoted to you when they sought your custom.
- Veterinary students work hard and like to play hard as well. Set yourself a limit on how much you are prepared to spend each term. Remember – the more partying, the worse your bank account will look. Perhaps you will go to the annual vet ball. If you do, why not consider buying the gear second hand? By all means join the Association of Veterinary Students (AVS), but do you want to attend the congress or go on sports weekends? They all cost money.
- Easter is a time when it is possible for students to augment their income. Once you have gained experience with your first lambing, students say that it is possible, if you are lucky, to make over £300

per week. This is very hard work involving 12 hours a day, for seven days a week, for a minimum of three weeks. But it will certainly improve the look of your bank account – and give you valuable experience.

International students

Students from outside the EU pay more in tuition fees than UK or EU students. The fees are £19,320 per year for pre-clinical and clinical training (based on figures provided by the RVC for 2010/11). International bursaries (based on the admissions process) to the value of one year's tuition fees are available.

Bursaries and grants

The veterinary schools offer bursaries and further advice on sources of funding. You should read the websites of the universities in order to find out whether you will be able to get a reduction in fees. The RVC, for example, offers a means-tested bursary (see Table 4 on page 33) and merit-based scholarships based on a number of indicators, including the interview and test scores.

Armed Forces bursaries are grants to selected veterinary students who pass their Army Officer Selection Board examinations and apply before their final university year. In return you have to spend four years in the service.

Otherwise, students are able to apply for student loans by selecting option 02 for Local Government Authority on the UCAS form under Fees and Funding. You can also apply to the Student Loans Company for a loan.

Finally, students should visit the British Veterinary Association (BVA) website to find out more about loans for veterinary students: www.bva.co.uk/public/documents/funding_sources.pdf.

Expected student expenditure

The lists on pages 32 and 34, taken from the website of the Faculty of Biology, University of Cambridge, show the estimated additional course costs (2009/10) for students applying to veterinary science courses at that institution.

Table 2 Student numbers 2010/11

University		First year admissions		Second year admissions (or later)		Admissions with a degree		Total number on course		Number taking intercalated course		Number holding intercalated degree		Number graduating (2005)	
		Male	Female	Male	Female	Male	Female	Male	Female	Male	Female	Male	Female	Male	Female
Bristol	UK	28	85	0	1	2	4	101	418	7	15	5	24	18	89
	EU	0	0	0	0	0	0	0	0	0	0	0	0	1	0
	Other	0	2	0	0	0	0	0	7	0	0	0	0	0	1
Cambridge	UK	21	51	1	5	1	5	97	387	1	3	5	3	21	88
	EU	0	0	0	0	0	0	0	4	0	0	0	0	0	1
	Other	0	2	0	0	0	0	2	8	0	0	0	0	0	0
Edinburgh	UK	23	64	5	11	7	15	108	387	1	3	5	3	21	88
	EU	0	3	3	2	3	4	11	21	0	0	0	0	1	1
	Other	5	19	9	36	12	42	29	130	0	1	0	3	2	0
Glasgow	UK	17	63	0	0	2	3	119	256	0	0	1	0	21	60
	EU	0	0	0	0	0	0	0	0	0	0	0	0	1	0
	Other	13	42	0	0	11	39	49	164	1	0	1	0	0	17
Liverpool	UK	24	75	4	11	4	13	112	440	1	7	13	19	36	86
	EU	0	1	0	0	1	0	1	5	1	0	0	0	0	1
	Other	0	2	0	0	0	2	1	5	0	0	0	0	0	1
London	UK	36	137	9	46	10	54	203	864	1	2	1	11	36	189
	EU	0	3	1	1	1	3	5	15	0	1	0	1	1	4
	Other	8	24	0	1	7	22	21	75	0	0	0	1	1	11
Nottingham	UK	24	60	0	0	1	3	84	238	n/a	n/a	n/a	n/a	n/a	n/a
	EU	4	2	0	0	1	0	5	9	n/a	n/a	n/a	n/a	n/a	n/a
	Other	3	5	0	0	0	1	4	16	n/a	n/a	n/a	n/a	n/a	n/a
Total		206	640	32	114	63	210	952	3449	13	32	31	66	160	637

Table 3 Expenditure estimate per pre-clinical year

Expenses	London (£)	Living away from home (£)	Living at home (£)
Tuition fees	3,290	3,290	3,290
Overalls	55	40	40
Lab coats	50	35	35
Wellies	35	35	35
Course notes	75	75	75
Textbooks	300	300	300
Travel costs	420	365	365
EMS travel costs	310	290	290
Student vet sub	60	60	60
Social events	1,200	1,200	950
Accommodation	4,000	3,500	N/A
Total	9,795	9,190	5,440

No tuition fees are payable by Scottish students in Scotland. Non-UK European Union students studying in Scotland pay £1,470 less in tuition fees.
Note: these figures, aside from the tuition fees which are applicable as of 2010/11 entry, were estimated in September 2010 and are intended only as a guide. Therefore, please refer to university websites for a detailed breakdown of the individual expenditure requirements.

Vets

- A Criminal Records Bureau (CRB) check (enhanced disclosure) is required before admission: £36
- Lab coat: £12.50
- Dissection kit, gloves, safety glasses, loan of locker and key, loan of dog skeleton: £22
- Veterinary dissection manual:* £11
- Course guides for neurobiology and comparative veterinary biology:* £6
- Wellington boots: £12
- University approved calculator: £10
- Electron micrographs (optional): £2
- Boiler suit: £25
- Extra Mural Studies (EMS) – 12 weeks required by the Royal College of Veterinary Surgeons (RCVS): variable depending on chosen placements
- British Veterinary Association (BVA) insurance cover: £27 per annum, but this will be met by the veterinary school.

*The manuals essentially replace the need for a textbook of human or veterinary anatomy.

Table 4 New entrants to veterinary medicine 2010/11: maintenance support

Family income (£)	Assessed family contribution	Maintenance grant	RVC bursary	Grant/bursary total	Maintenance loan (max. £6,928*)	Grant, loan & bursary total
25,000	0	2,906	1,650	4,556	5,475	10,031
30,000	0	1,906	1,082	2,988	5,975	8,963
34,400	0	1,106	628	1,734	6,375	8,109
39,333	0	755	429	1,184	6,551	7,735
40,000	0	711	0	711	6,573	7,284
45,000	0	381	0	381	6,738	7,119
50,020	0	50	0	50	6,903	6,953
50,778	0	0	0	0	6,928	6,928
55,000	844	0	0	0	6,084	6,084
60,000	1,844	0	0	0	5,084	5,084
60,478	1,940	0	0	0	4,988 (†)	4,988
65,000	1,940	0	0	0	4,988	4,988

Reprinted with kind permission from the RVC website: www.rvc.ac.uk/Undergraduate/Finances.cfm

Key

* Maximum loan calculated for a standard academic year. Courses at the RVC are often slightly longer and extra weeks payments are added to this amount.

† This is the point at which the 72% non-means tested element of the loan is recorded.

Veterinary medicine (clinical)

- Overalls: £25
- Boots: £12
- Stethoscope: £4.20
- EMS – 26 weeks required by RCVS: variable depending on chosen placements
- Grants available to assist with cost of BVA insurance cover: £27 per annum but this will be met by the veterinary school.

Case study

Daniel is in the fourth year of his veterinary studies. He has opted to follow a six-year course which incorporates an intercalated BSc degree. His third year involved research projects in other departments of the university, and he gained a BSc in Anatomy. The reason that Daniel chose the intercalated BSc course is that his interests lie in the field of veterinary research rather than practice. He has a particular interest in equine medicine and behaviour, and chose his university because of its strong links with an equine hospital.

Daniel gained nine A grades at GCSE, and chose to study Biology, Chemistry, Physics and Psychology at A level. 'My interest was always in the theoretical side of practical work at school. I was always breaking things and my experiments would never work. It became a joke amongst my teachers and the others in my classes. When I told them that I wanted to study veterinary science at university, it caused great hilarity. My careers teacher gave me lots of help in preparing for my interviews, and we decided that the best option was to be very honest about my interest in research rather than try to pretend that I wanted to be a practising vet. Most of my work experience was in research. My school helped me to arrange some placements at Birmingham University during my A levels, working with postgraduates on molecular biology, and I was able to bring along reports to my interviews. I managed to get four A grades at A level, but it was a close run thing because I didn't get high marks in my biology and chemistry coursework, and my physics practical exam was a disaster. The veterinary course is very practically focused and I have discovered that I enjoy this more than I thought I would. Not enough to make me want to change direction, though! My aim is to work in a university research department, and possibly in a pharmaceutical company later on.'

Most of Daniel's friends on the veterinary course want to work as veterinary surgeons. They particularly enjoy the practical side of the course, but can sometimes find the theoretical aspects difficult because they seem less relevant to the realities of working as a practising vet. 'Despite the different directions that we want to take in our careers,' says Daniel, 'we have one thing in common – we are all absolutely focused on our goals, and we work incredibly hard in order to achieve these. Studying veterinary science is demanding – I am sometimes jealous of friends studying arts subjects at the university because they have so much free time. They also have more money than I do because they all have part-time jobs – something I don't have time to do. However, they do not have clear ideas about where their lives are heading, which I do. I wouldn't swap places with them.'

5 | Take the bull by the horns in the cattle market
Applying to veterinary school

Admissions tutors try to get the best students they can for their course. That is putting it at its most basic. But there is more to it than that. They are also acting in the best interests of the veterinary profession. They know that the competition is fierce and that the biggest hurdle faced by aspiring students is entry into a veterinary school. Once this obstacle is overcome there is, given the undoubted ability of those able enough to get the entry grades needed, every chance that with diligence and lots of hard work the student will in due course enter the profession.

However, it is important to understand that motivation is the key factor in selection. It is, in the last analysis, more important even than A levels or their equivalent. Therefore, admissions tutors look at the total impression conveyed by the candidate in their UCAS application. This will include not only academic predictions and head teacher's report but also extracurricular interests as well as the extremely important supporting practical experience and references. Admissions tutors know that they are exercising a big responsibility: their decisions will largely shape the future profession.

Taking a broad view

Ideally, admissions tutors will seek to have students representing a good cross-section of the community. In recent years more women are applying and being admitted than men. Then there is the question of background. Those with an upbringing in country areas can have an excellent range of experience and general knowledge of animal husbandry. Some of them may be the sons or daughters of farmers or vets. Clearly they have a lot to offer. Yet it would be unfair and divisive to fill a course with people who all had these advantages. What of the students coming from the cities where gaining practical experience is not so easy?

A few places will be kept for graduates taking veterinary science as a second degree. There will also be some places reserved for overseas students who provide valuable income as well as added richness to the mix of students in all the veterinary schools. Nevertheless, the overwhelming majority of places on these courses will be filled by school-leavers or those who have taken a year out since leaving school.

Academic versus practical

As mentioned in Chapter 2, most of the veterinary schools require a minimum of six weeks' work experience made up in the way described above. However, despite the strong emphasis on practical experience demanded by all the veterinary schools, many people in the veterinary profession are concerned that the high A level grades required, currently ranging between A*AA and AAB, suggest that the profession is being filled with people who, while being academically very bright, are not so hot dealing with the practical side of the work. Apart from the fact that it is often wrong to assume that academically able people are always very impractical, this trend reveals an imperfect understanding of the logistics of the UCAS operation each year and how the admissions tutors in the veterinary schools deal with it. The UCAS application and the supporting evidence of motivation are crucial to understanding what happens.

Professor Gaskell, when he was Dean of Liverpool's Veterinary School, left no room for doubt that the most important thing from the admissions point of view is understanding what the prospective student is about and his or her motivation. This has to come across in the student's UCAS application. But that is not to say academic ability is unimportant. There is an enormous amount that has to be learned, and Professor Gaskell advises, 'It's the same with medicine – we find that A levels or their equivalent are good indicators of the ability to absorb, hold and recall information.'

The problem with weaker A levels is that you may start to find the amount of learning required difficult. Fortunately, veterinary science is in the position of being able to select the best of the motivated. It must be added that it is not in the interests of the profession, or the animals and their owners whom the vets serve, to relax this strong position.

Open days

You should visit the veterinary schools that hold special interest for you on their open day. Such a visit will give you the chance to see some of the work of the veterinary school. There will be special exhibits, possibly a video programme and most probably the chance to hear the views of the admissions tutor. There may also be the opportunity to visit the veterinary school's own field station where most of the clinical work is done in the final stages of the course, and although veterinary students are kept very busy you may get the chance to speak with some of them. Some schools actually arrange for a number of their students to accompany parties of visitors on the open day. The open day will also give you an opportunity to see the general attractions of each university as a place to live and study over the next five (or six) years.

As with most things nowadays, everything you need to know is on the internet, so your first point of call must be the individual university websites to look for updated information on their open days. Your school will also receive details of open days with forms to be completed by those wishing to attend. If you have not heard by about a month ahead of the college open day you wish to attend, make enquiries in your school's careers department. If you hear nothing you should take the initiative yourself and write to the school liaison office or directly to the address of the institution which interests you. (See the contact information in Chapter 10.) You owe it to yourself to find out as much as you can. Your visit and how you felt about it could be a talking point should you be called for interview. So do not squander the opportunity to fit one or two visits into your A level study schedule.

If you are taking time out gaining practical experience and have already met the academic requirements, you may be able to get away to attend more open days. If this is the case you may find that you receive more than one unconditional offer and so you should certainly try to visit as many of these events as you can to help you make the best decision.

It is a good idea to make notes after each visit to an open day of your impressions and what differences you spotted. These notes will be very useful if you are called for interview when you will almost certainly be asked about your visit.

Course entry requirements

The academic requirements of the seven veterinary schools are similar, but there are some differences, and it is important that you obtain the most up-to-date information before deciding where to apply.

You can get information from:

- university prospectuses
- university websites (more likely to be up to date)
- HEAP 2012: University Degree Course Offers by Brian Heap (Trotman Publishing, publication date May 2011)
- university admissions staff.

Typical student offers for the academic year 2010/11 are listed in Table 1 on page 28.

For A level students, the selectors will take into account:

- GCSE grades
- AS choices and grades
- A level (A2) choices and predictions/grades
- documentation on any extenuating circumstances that might have affected your performance.

You will be asked for 'good grades at GCSE'. This means lots of A and A* grades, particularly in the sciences, English and mathematics. If you did not get good GCSE grades, you can still apply for veterinary science, but your referee should make it clear why you did not achieve the grades that you needed – there may have been circumstances, such as illness, which affected your performance.

Every university student has to meet the general matriculation requirements of each university (consult the prospectuses for details), but in addition there is the special prescribed subject requirement. You should check the requirements carefully – the veterinary schools' websites carry the most up-to-date information – but it is likely that you will need three A levels (that is, three subjects carried to A2 level), which will include Chemistry, Biology and one other science/mathematical subject. Your choice of AS and A level subjects is vital because although one veterinary school might require three sciences (including Chemistry) at AS level with two taken on to A2 level, others will require Biology and Chemistry at A2, or even three sciences at A2. If you are applying to Cambridge, you should be aware that different colleges have different requirements. Currently, no veterinary school makes a conditional offer on three A levels at below AAB grades. Unlike the requirements for many other courses, offers are likely to be made on the basis of A level grades only: stand-alone AS levels are unlikely to be taken into account. However, clearly the AS grades are important because they will be stated on the UCAS application, and thus will give the admissions tutors an indication that you are on course for AAA or AAB at A level. For example, when faced with two candidates whose academic backgrounds are identical except that one has AAAA at AS level whereas the other has CCCC, who do you think they would favour?

The A* system is still something of an unknown quantity and only Cambridge demand it as part of their requirements at undergraduate level – A*AA. This grade is still considered by the other universities to be the equivalent of an A grade.

Some students have been known to query whether they should take a fifth AS level or a fourth A level (not including General Studies). Before taking another subject you should bear in mind that if you offer four A levels your performance in all four subjects will be taken into account.

So if you do feel inclined to add a fourth subject at A level, remember the high grades needed for admission.

Other qualifications

For applicants with **Scottish qualifications**, it is likely that you will be asked for AAABB or higher in your Higher grades (SCE/SQA) and Advanced Higher grades in Chemistry and at least one other science subject. Some veterinary schools like candidates to take a new subject at Higher level if only two Advanced Higher grade subjects are taken in the sixth year. Higher grades alone are unlikely to be sufficient.

The **Irish Leaving Certificate** is unlikely to be accepted as equivalent to GCE A level. This is because studying a wider range of subjects to a lower or less specific level than the UK's A levels does not meet the need of the veterinary science course requirements. Therefore, this qualification must be offered in combination with UK qualifications.

The **International Baccalaureate** is usually acceptable, provided that appropriate combinations of subjects are studied. Three subjects are needed at the Higher Level. They must include chemistry and biology, as well as ideally one or both of physics and mathematics. Grade scores needed in the Higher Level are likely to be 7, 7 and 6. If the combination is likely to be different, advice should be sought. Similar subject combinations are required by those offering the **European Baccalaureate**. Applicants are likely to need an average score of 8.0, including Chemistry and Biology.

The **Advanced Diploma** in the following subjects will be considered at Grade A alongside A levels in Biology and Chemistry (only at the RVC): business; administration and finance; construction and the built environment; creative and media; engineering; environmental and land-based studies; hair and beauty studies; hospitality; information technology; manufacturing and product design; society, health and development.

Access to HE Diplomas must include a minimum of 15 Level 3 credits in Biology, and 15 Level 3 credits in Chemistry. These must also be Distinctions in all modules taken.

Admissions tests

Applicants to certain medicine, veterinary medicine and related courses are required to take the BioMedical Admissions Test (BMAT). The BMAT is owned and administered by Cambridge Assessment, one of the world's largest assessment agencies. Time is the biggest factor in these admissions tests: there are a lot of questions and you don't have a lot of time to complete them. Of the seven UK veterinary schools, the test is currently required by Bristol, Cambridge and the Royal Veterinary College in London. Have a go at the question below (the answer is on page 47).

Sample BMAT question

Doctors in Great Britain can work for the public health service, a commercial service, or both. Thirty per cent of doctors in Great Britain work, at least some of the time, for the commercial sector. On the basis of this information alone, deduce which of the following statements are true of doctors in Great Britain.

1 Some doctors work only in the public health service.
2 More doctors work in the public health service than the commercial sector.
3 Some doctors spend more time on commercial work than in the public health service.

A 1 only
B 2 only
C 1 and 2 only
D 2 and 3 only
E 1, 2 and 3

From the specimen papers available on the Cambridge Assessment website (www.admissionstests.cambridgeassessment.org.uk). Reprinted by permission of the University of Cambridge Local Examinations Syndicate.

Graduates from other countries

It is possible to practise as a vet in the UK having studied overseas. The process is simpler for students who have studied in the EU, or in certain universities in Canada, Australia, South Africa or New Zealand. However, graduates from other countries can still practise in the UK if they pass the Statutory Examination for Membership of the RCVS, which is held in a UK veterinary school in May/June each year. Further information for all overseas graduates can be obtained from the RCVS website (www.rcvs.org.uk).

Studying outside the UK

An option open to students who wish to study overseas, but want to undertake some of their clinical training in one of the UK veterinary schools, is the veterinary science course offered by St George's University in Grenada, West Indies. For contact details for the course, see Chapter 10.

Submitting your application

Applications for admission to veterinary science degree courses have to be made through UCAS. Applications for veterinary science must be received by UCAS by 15 October for entry in the following year. Applications received after this may be considered by the veterinary schools, but they are not bound to do so, and given the number of applications that they will receive, it is likely that they will not do so. In order to ensure that your application reaches UCAS by the deadline, you should complete it at least two weeks before this date so that your referee has time to write his or her report. The current UCAS application should be available via your school or college. However, if you have left school, or have any difficulties accessing the electronic application system, you should write, after 1 July in the year preceding entry, to UCAS, Rosehill, New Barn Lane, Cheltenham, Gloucestershire GL52 3LZ.

Unlike in previous years, if you wish to apply to the University of Cambridge you are no longer required to complete the blue Preliminary Application Form (PAF). You will, however, be required to complete a Supplementary Application Questionnaire (SAQ), in keeping with the requirements of many other universities. More information on applications to Cambridge can be found in another book in this series, *Getting into Oxford & Cambridge*.

The table below forms part of a student survey published by the British Veterinary Association (BVA). The figures might be rough approximations this year, but in most years the split is considered to be 80% of female applicants to 20% of male applicants. Therefore, gents, there is a balance to be addressed here!

How many applications to make

You may only apply to four veterinary science courses. If you apply to more than four, your UCAS application will be returned, and by

Table 5 Number of male and female applicants

	All applicants	Degree accepts	Clearing accepts
Men	458	212	23
Women	1,522	673	82
Total	1,980	885	105

the time you amend it, you may well have missed the 15 October deadline.

A common question is: 'Should I put a non-veterinary science choice in the remaining slot?' There are arguments for and against doing so, and you will need to discuss this with your careers adviser or referee. It would probably not be a good idea to apply for veterinary nursing, for example, but it might make sense to apply for a course in equine science. The admissions staff at all of the veterinary schools emphasise that candidates will not be disadvantaged if they fill the remaining place with another course. However, you should be wary of putting down a course that you are not interested in, and accepting an offer as your insurance place, since you will not be eligible for Clearing if you do so.

Therefore, holding 'insurance' offers will depend on how committed you are to veterinary science. An argument in favour of going all out for the total commitment of applying solely to veterinary schools is that if you fall short of the required grades, and have just missed out, you will almost certainly have the option of gaining entry into an alternative course through Clearing. This is because other pure and applied science courses are invariably much less competitive and you will be able to accept an offer if you want to do so, although it is more likely to be at a lower-ranked institution.

However, if you decide to choose an alternative course as your insurance choice you should not put down medicine or dentistry. Although veterinary science admissions tutors would not automatically exclude anyone because of this mixture, they would certainly look long and hard for overwhelming evidence that veterinary science was what you really wanted. By the same token, you could hardly expect to satisfy the medical admissions tutors!

All things being equal, it seems logical for applications listing clearly related subjects in the D sector of UCAS – the sector detailing all animal-related studies such as agriculture, equine studies, animal physiology, biochemistry, microbiology or zoology – to possess that important quality of coherence and to fit in with the general thrust of your application.

Transferring from another degree

If you really want to become a veterinary surgeon, and with hard work you can attain the necessary academic standard, it is not a good idea to take a different degree. Some people are badly advised to do another degree and then try to transfer from another course into veterinary science. This is not feasible because it is necessary to study certain subjects which are exclusive to veterinary science from the beginning: examples are veterinary anatomy and ruminant physiology. In addition, the chance of there being extra places is remote. Transfer then becomes impossible and the only way you could proceed would be to go back and start your veterinary studies at the beginning. Therefore, no one should be advised to take a different course and then try to transfer. However, it is worth noting that Cambridge has been known to make some concessions to students wishing to transfer from mainly medically related degrees. Such students might, because of the Cambridge tripos system, be able to complete a veterinary science degree at the end of six or seven years' study, depending on when the transfer was made; but they will still need to study veterinary physiology and anatomy.

Further reasons why it might prove unwise to do a degree in another subject are that even if you become a graduate in another cognate sub-ject, with an upper second or even a first, your application could be assessed on the basis of your original A levels as well as the subsequent university study. This is done in fairness to the large number of school-leavers applying. A decisive argument for most people is that in nearly all these cases graduates in other subjects would only be admitted on a 'full cost' basis. Some colleges allocate a small number of places to gradu-ates within the home and EU intake. Tuition fees for these would usually be at full cost payable throughout the course. (However, fees at Not-tingham and the Royal Veterinary College for home graduates are cur-rently the same as for first-degree students.) There are no scholarships available for graduate applicants, with the possible exception of some Cambridge colleges or those that are privately funded.

Deferring entry and taking a gap year

The UCAS system permits you to apply at the start of Year 13 for entry a year after completion of your A levels. However, you will be expected to meet the conditions of the offer in the year of application. The major-ity of veterinary schools now welcome students deciding to postpone their entry to the course. The most common reasons given by students are the opportunity to travel, study or work abroad, or gain additional relevant experience for the course and profession they seek to enter. The latter reason is the one most likely to influence veterinary schools because many applicants do need to strengthen their range of relevant work experience.

You should be able to explain your plans for the year taken out. Does it involve some animal experience? Those coming from urban areas may find that undertaking a gap year of a relevant nature is slightly more difficult to achieve. It is a good idea to discuss this matter on an informal basis with an admissions tutor and get some advice.

A level predictions

As has already been indicated, performance in A levels (or equivalent exams) is not the sole determinant in selection because of the importance of other motivational factors. However, predicted A level performance is an important factor for admissions tutors in sifting through and finding committed candidates likely to meet the stipulated academic level. Final decisions are made when A level results are known.

It is at this point that some rejected applicants will do better than predicted. When the admissions tutors learn that a rejected candidate has achieved top grades and is excellent in other respects, they have been known to change the original rejection to an unconditional acceptance for the following year. Over 100 places are settled each year in this way. Indeed, the majority of entrants to veterinary science courses will have taken a year out, whether they intended to or not. Those whose grades slip slightly below their conditional offer will usually be considered in August and could be offered entry if places are available. The importance, therefore, of A levels is that once the results are known, the tutors can announce the final decisions that have been made concerning the group of well-motivated and committed preselected candidates.

In certain cases, if applicants have met and exceeded the grades asked of them by a veterinary school they are eligible to enter Adjustment through UCAS. However, it's extremely unlikely that the applicant would be able to find another course in veterinary medicine, and once they have committed to a course through Adjustment they must stick to their decision.

Case study

Alice is studying veterinary medicine in London. She was unsuccessful in her first application. 'I really was not prepared well enough for my application. This was my fault rather than my school's, because the school didn't have any experience of veterinary applications. I should have taken the whole process much more seriously. I had wanted to be a vet from the age of about 14, although probably for the wrong reasons. I loved my pets and, like most girls of that age, wanted to own a horse. My school gave me advice about the AS and A levels to choose, and showed me where the prospectuses and university guides were in the careers room. I had an idea that work experience was important but, living in central London, my opportunities were limited. I got a Saturday job in a pet shop, and I hoped that this would be sufficient. I got eight A or A* grades at GCSE and I was predicted A grades in all my A level subjects, and I was very surprised when I was rejected by all four vet schools. It was only at that point that I realised how serious I was about becoming a vet.

'I discussed the situation with my family and they agreed to me taking a gap year and reapplying. This time I did my research. I arranged a variety of work experience placements, using the vet school prospectuses and websites to guide me as to what was needed. I went to open days and tried to talk to as many students as possible about their applications in order to make sure I was as well prepared as they had been. I also made a point of reading as widely as possible about veterinary-related issues in preparation for the interview. To be honest, if I had got an interview the first time I almost certainly would have been rejected because I would not have been able to answer most of the questions convincingly. In retrospect, being rejected in my first application was a good thing, because it helped me to realise how committed I needed to be in order to be successful as a vet.'

Answer to sample question on page 42: C

6 | No one likes a copy cat
The personal statement

Gone are the days of pen and paper. The UCAS application is filled in via the UCAS website, so you can no longer rely on the size of your handwriting to cram in every last possible word. There is a 4,000-character limit (including spaces), which equates roughly to 47 lines. So remember, be concise in what you want to convey and try to be unique.

Importance of the personal statement

The personal statement may be the last part of the UCAS application you fill in, but it is certainly the most important and influential. Most of the information you supply via UCAS is a factual summary of what you have achieved, but in the personal statement you have your first chance to give expression, clarity and style to your application and hence bid for a place at veterinary school.

Make sure you plan your statement carefully. Remember that brevity can often produce a better, more directed answer. Word-process the statement first and then cut it down to within the maximum number of characters if necessary. Research shows that it is a good idea to structure your response. Consider using subheadings to give clarity for the busy admissions tutor, and make sure that the following points are covered in your personal statement.

- Why do you want to be a veterinary surgeon? There are many possible reasons and this is where your individuality will show.
- Outline your practical experience. Give prominence to the diverse nature of it, the clinics, farms, stables, etc. you have worked at or visited.
- Mention any specific interesting cases that you witnessed or assisted with.
- You like animals, but how do you respond to people?
- How did you get on with vets, nurses and the customers? Any teamwork experience?
- Give an indication of your career direction, even if it is tentative at this stage. Show that you have thought about the possibilities.

- Have you had any special achievements or responsibilities connected either with animals or with an outside interest?
- List other activities and interests of a social, cultural or sporting kind. Here is your chance to reveal more about yourself as an individual.
- Finally, remember to keep a copy of your personal statement before you pass it on to your referee. The copy will serve to refresh your memory before you are called for interviews.

The example personal statements below show how an applicant might structure their personal statement. The first example illustrates an old-fashioned but methodical approach to writing a personal statement and will always be useful as a template for your own statement. The other examples are different in their own ways: for instance, the second focuses primarily on work experience, whereas in the third, as well as detailing their work experience, the applicant has also shown an appreciation of different issues affecting vets in practice today.

It is impossible to pick one of these personal statements as the definitive article because they are all individual. There are no right or wrong answers, only a correct template/model to use. As long as the personal statement is personal and means something to you, you will have achieved your goal.

Quotes are only desirable in a personal statement if you can link them to the point that you are trying to make.

Remember: be concise and try to be unique.

Example personal statement 1 (3,090 characters with spaces)

My determination to study veterinary medicine has been reinforced by my work experience with both large and small animals. I find working with animals hugely rewarding and I have always had a strong interest in their care and welfare. Veterinary medicine would give me further opportunities to pursue my interest in science, and apply my knowledge to tackle a wide variety of problems in diagnosis, treatment and research. Veterinary medicine combines all aspects that I would look for in a vocation, including working closely with people and working as part of a team. Below is a summary of my work experience to date:

- one week at Glades Veterinary Surgery (small animal)
- one week at Hunters House Veterinary Surgery (mixed practice)

- two weeks at Equine Veterinary Practice
- one week at the Blue Cross
- three weeks at Hayes Park Dairy Farm, including calving
- one and a half weeks at Crocketts Farm (public), including lambing
- two weeks at Forest Stables
- three years at Slemans Barn Farm (stables)
- one year at Bilbow Stables
- one day at Smith's Abattoir.

At Hayes Park, I was able to take an active role in all aspects of calf husbandry and found the hands-on and practical nature of the work very appealing. Working at the farm also highlighted the difficulty farmers have in balancing commercial and welfare aspects in farming. This was particularly evident during the foot-and-mouth crisis where it appeared that many of these problems can be due to commercial pressures, such as ever-decreasing market value of livestock. Whilst working at Crocketts Farm I worked with a variety of animals, from rabbits and guinea pigs to zebu and llamas. This work also included lambing, often in front of the general public. I frequently had to answer questions about what was happening and explain my actions. This customer aspect of the work was very satisfying. The time I spent in local veterinary practices allowed me to assist and watch both basic and more complex surgical procedures. I found it fascinating being able to watch an endoscopy being carried out on the oesophagus of a horse and I was able to relate my knowledge of biology to what I was seeing. My equine veterinary experience showed me how I could combine my love of horses with a career in veterinary medicine. I also enjoyed participating in the Vetsim and Vetsix courses.

Interests and responsibilities

Horse riding (I own a 7-year-old gelding and am actively involved in all aspects of his care and schooling); Duke of Edinburgh Award Scheme (achieved the Bronze and Silver and currently completing the Gold Award); Manston Drama Club (local theatre group – I played lead in last production); music (Grade 4 piano, Grade 5 flute and currently working towards Grade 5 theory); School Prefect.

Following my exams, I have arranged to travel to South Africa for three months. I will spend my time teaching in local primary schools for under-privileged children and working in the Simbari game reserve. The game reserve activities include wildlife veterinary work, game monitoring and assisting with guests at the Game Lodge.

Example personal statement 2 (3,685 characters with spaces)

I have always had an interest in the care of animals and the work experience I have completed has proved to me that the profession of veterinary medicine is one which I would like to follow. At 14, I volunteered at my local Blue Cross Centre for a year to improve my understanding of animals. Since then I have undertaken work experience to deepen my knowledge of a career as a vet. I have visited small animal surgeries: the Wheelhouse in Chesham and the Park Vets in Watford. I also completed work experience at Wendover Heights small animal surgery, where I saw a rare case of 'rubber jaw' in a short-haired dachshund. I came to appreciate the variety of roles a vet performs, from routine examinations to dealing with difficult ethical issues, and I saw how vital it is to be able to communicate with owners and to establish a trusting relationship with them. I also gained experience at Hampden Vets large animal veterinary surgery where I was allowed to join the vet on-call. I really enjoyed the farm work experience that I undertook, which has made me think that I may like to take the route of a large animal vet, although I will keep my options open.

To further advance my understanding of different varieties of animals I worked on a public farm for two weeks at Odds Farm and have completed 12 weeks' basic farm husbandry at a holiday complex in Cornwall. I also visited a battery chicken farm for a day and completed two days' lambing on a non-organic farm and one day's lambing on an organic farm in Cornwall. In addition, I was given the opportunity to shadow a vet at an abattoir, which was very interesting as I saw the effect that a recent foot-and-mouth outbreak had on the abattoir.

After my exams in January I am going to help with calving at a farm near Harefield for a week and then I intend to apply for a job at a local kennels. I can also speak fluent German so I have organised a week of work experience at a veterinary hospital in Germany in February to see how the veterinary profession differs to that of the UK's, followed by volunteering at an animal shelter. I have also received a work experience placement at Battersea Children's Zoo for the summer.

The veterinary profession requires interpersonal and teamwork skills. I feel I have achieved these through completing the Bronze, Silver and Gold Duke of Edinburgh Awards. Through this award I learnt new skills, such as sea kayaking, as my Gold Expedition was to kayak across Scotland and gained a three-star award. As part of my residential section I volunteered on a steam railway in north Wales. I showed I can adapt to new surroundings and can work well with other people and members of the public. I am currently working towards my Grade 8 flute and have played in the school orchestra and concert band for several years. I received the art scholarship at my secondary school and I particularly enjoy fine art drawing which has improved my dexterity skills. I have practised horse riding for the past 11 years and have a great understanding for horses and the care they require. I attended VetCam at the University of Cambridge and Vetsim at Nottingham University. Both of these courses helped me see what the veterinary profession requires and it strengthened my determination. I also completed a marine mammal medic course.

I enjoy reading the 'New Scientist' and 'UK Vet' magazines which, together with my A level subjects of Chemistry, Biology and Mathematics, has given me a firm scientific foundation upon which to build in future. The work experience I have undertaken has allowed me to confirm my desire to study veterinary medicine and this determination shows my commitment to the subject.

Example personal statement 3 (3,974 characters with spaces)

The American Vet, Richard H. Pitcairn, once said that, 'living with animals can be a wonderful experience, especially if we choose to learn the valuable lessons animals teach through their natural enthusiasm, grace, resourcefulness, affection and forgiveness', and this is something that I feel that I have learned through my personal experiences with animals.

I have always been interested in the sciences; my interest in veterinary science was fuelled further in school while studying the interactions between the human body and drugs such as the pharmacological action of optical isomers and in turn relating those same situations to animals. The study of the human anatomy has always held interest to me and I am keen to develop my understanding into the animal world.

David Grant at the RSPCA Harmsworth Memorial Hospital, was quoted in the 'Guardian' in 2007 as saying that, 'when animals become a fashion accessory, cruelty is never far behind', which ties in with my overriding aim to reduce the suffering of any animal and improve their quality of life. I understand and appreciate the value of animals in our world today. Witnessing euthanasia in my first ever veterinary consultation showed me the immediate difficulty of being a vet in practice. The vet in question displayed complete professionalism, showing how being a vet requires more than just knowing the theory behind the practice. Spending a further two weeks on a farm in south-west Wales during the lambing season gave a valuable insight to how a vet's clientele work. I became aware of the concept of prophylaxis and the importance of biosurveillance and biosecurity on agricultural sites to aid in the prevention of the spread of disease. The farm was another world from the comfort of the centrally heated veterinary surgery and I felt a greater sense of personal satisfaction being involved in the daily routine. Whilst in Wales I went to observe the happenings at a slaughter house, just to see what happens at the other end of the spectrum, something I believe all vets need to detach themselves from.

I was fortunate enough to spend time with the aforementioned David Grant at the RSPCA Harmsworth Memorial Hospital and a week spent on a game reserve helping with the capture and release of sable antelope. Working with David, about whom I had read so much, was a fantastic experience and it gave me the opportunity to discuss with him the problem of the increasingly popular world of organised dog fighting, on which he lectures. It was evident he loved and relished in the challenges he was presented with every day and being in the presence of that passion was truly inspiring. My most recent experience was two weeks with a country vet in Cashel. This was the hardest experience so far – some shifts were even as long as 12 hours – and successfully diagnosing and treating animals' results in this environment proved very rewarding.

From my work experience I have learnt the true responsibility and nature of being a vet. Whether working in a practice or on a farm, it requires a huge amount of patience, sympathy and practical ability. Even brief contact with animals can create an immediate emotional bond. Understanding the enormously strong relationship between an owner and their animal and indeed respecting that bond, is a vital part of being a vet. If nothing else this work has shown me that communication and emotional distance are key.

At Mill Hill I was awarded the title of Head of House and played representative rugby for many years, captaining the 1st XV and playing for Saracens RFC. I am also a senior NCO in the CCF, from which I have gained improved communication and interpersonal skills.

On a basic level, a vet must realise that every animal is unique. The fact that each case presented is different offers me the type of challenge that I relish and being able to successfully diagnose and treat an animal in a case-by-case situation is, to me, certainly something special.

Example personal statement 4 (3,961 characters with spaces)

I have always had an interest in the care and welfare of animals. When I was younger I helped feed a rejected lamb and it was then that I realised that I wanted to work in veterinary medicine. However, I took many decisions that led to that not being the career I pursued, but after maturing and gaining the experience and some of the skills necessary for being a vet I believe I am now in a position to enter into training to become a vet and feel I would be a valuable asset to this profession. Veterinary medicine allows for the diagnosis and care of animals, however it also has many other facets that interest me such as working with people, communication and being part of a team. I feel that as a mature student I can bring these skills and many others that I have gained from previous experience to the profession of veterinary medicine. The work experience I have undertaken has reinforced to me that veterinary medicine is the profession I want to pursue.

I volunteer every Sunday at Tropical Wings World of Wildlife, where I work with the keepers in every aspect of animal care and husbandry from helping clean enclosures to feeding and handling the animals. I have worked with many animals that are not commonly encountered such as otters, wallabies and meerkats, as well as more common household animals such as rabbits and guinea pigs as well as larger animals such as horses and goats. I also work with the public helping out at animal encounters and assisting with birthday parties where the children can meet and handle the animals; this has improved my interpersonal and communication skills further.

I did a week's work experience at my local veterinary practice where I observed and assisted in some operations, sat in on consultations and got a general view of how a veterinary practice works and the different roles in a practice. During my time there I assisted with an endoscopy on a West Highland terrier, saw the removal of a large tumour from an anaesthetised guinea pig, the removal of a toe from a Doberman and a partial ear removal from a dog. I also observed many common operations such as spaying, castrations and teeth extractions. I also saw a cat being euthanised: although this was a hard experience to witness, due to the owner's distress, the cat was very unwell and any more treatment would not have helped so it was best to put it to sleep. This experience showed me a hard but necessary part of veterinary medicine as it demonstrated that the animal's welfare must go above the emotion people have towards their pets. The consultations allowed me to observe how vets interact with owners as well as the animals and offered valuable insight into the veterinary career.

My family has a history of farming and I spent a lot of Easters on my uncle's farm when I was younger. This was during the lambing season and I assisted when occasionally a lamb had to be hand reared. More recently I spent a week on my uncle's turkey farm where they intensively farm turkeys. This offered a different perspective to the veterinary practice as the difference between seeing animals as pets and seeing them as a way of life as well as a livelihood, is something I have always been aware of.

I visited an abattoir in October. This helped to see all aspects of farming as it followed on from what I had experienced at my uncle's farm. I believe it is an essential part of a veterinarian's work to understand the needs of a client, and farmers have very different needs for their animals than are experienced in a small-animal veterinary practice.

My work experience has shown me that whether on a farm, a veterinary practice or a zoo a vet requires many skills such as communication, empathy, teamwork and practical ability. I feel that being a mature student I bring with me these skills and others such as reacting well under pressure, how I interact with the public and colleagues as well as determination to succeed in my chosen profession.

Referee's report

After you have completed the declaration, your application is ready to be passed to your referee for completion. They will then send it to UCAS. The referee is usually someone who knows you better than anyone else in your school/college, someone who can draw upon the opinions of other members of staff and information contained in the school records. In schools this is most likely to be your form tutor, whereas in colleges it will probably be your director of studies. However, mature students or graduates for whom school was too long ago for such a reference to be meaningful should approach people who know them well. A good idea is to consider asking someone for whom they have recently worked.

References are an important factor since they provide insight into your character and personality. They can also provide significant confirmation of career aims, achievements and interests. The referee's view of your abilities, in terms of analysis, powers of expression and willingness to question things, is the kind of independent information about you that will have an influence with selectors. Additional information about family circumstances and health problems, which candidates rarely offer about themselves, will also be taken into account.

Other supporting documentation

Because work experience in veterinary practices and farms is so important in the selection of applicants for veterinary school, you will be expected to list full details of all such experience. Some veterinary schools will send you a questionnaire asking you to expand on the information you gave about work experience in your UCAS application. Applicants can expect interested veterinary schools to follow up by writing to the veterinary practices and farms where you have worked for additional information about you (this information will be confidential). This is a good sign as it shows that your application has aroused more than a passing interest.

In essence, the veterinary school will ask whether the people you have worked with regard you as a suitable entrant into the veterinary profession. The sorts of issues that concern tutors are:

- general enthusiasm
- ability to express yourself clearly
- helpfulness
- practical ability
- attitude to the animals, to customers and to clerical and nursing staff in the practice – in other words, were you a pleasure to have around?

So it is clear that the veterinary school can take steps to get hold of additional information about you. You can also help yourself by taking the initiative to gain documentary support. For example, once you have received your UCAS acknowledgement and application number, you can ask your local vet to write to the veterinary school(s) of your choice (quoting your application number), giving details of the work that you did there with extra details on any interesting cases with which you were involved. This information will go into your file and is bound to help, especially if the vet is able to say that he or she 'would like to see this person in veterinary school'.

There are exceptions to this arrangement. For instance, the Royal Veterinary College would prefer that you bring copies of all supporting statements, references and casebooks to your interview rather than sending them in advance. It would therefore be wise to contact the individual schools to which you are applying to enquire whether they have any preference regarding how they receive additional statements supporting work experience.

Mature students

In view of the extreme competition it is unrealistic for mature students, at say age 25–30 years, to expect special treatment. They should expect to satisfy the academic entry requirements in the usual way at one recent sitting and must have a good range of practical experience. However, this requirement has been known to be waived in exceptional cases, such as where a mature student displays strong motivation coupled with academic ability.

Mature applicants should use the personal statement section of the UCAS application to set out their qualifications and work experience. Your objective is to signal to the admissions tutors why they should see you. Your extra maturity and practical experience should show here. If you cannot get all the information in the space allowed, make sure you summarise what you want to get across in accordance with the bullet points at the start of the chapter – why you want to study veterinary science, what you have done to explore this decision, how you respond to people, how you react under pressure, what your career aspirations are and what your extracurricular interests are in order to show that you are a rounded individual.

Remember, it is very important to show why you want to work with animals and to give details of any relevant work experience of a paid or voluntary nature. If you feel that the space in the personal statement section of the UCAS application does not permit you to do full justice to yourself, it is a good idea to prepare a curriculum vitae or further documentation and send this directly to the veterinary school with your UCAS application number.

What to do if you are rejected

Generally one of the main reasons for rejection is insufficient practical experience, particularly a lack of farm work. If this is true in your own case, you could try to remedy the deficiency between the A level examinations and the publication of the results. All applications are reconsidered after your A level results are known. If your academic results are satisfactory you may be offered a place for the subsequent year.

If you are rejected but have reached the necessary academic standard or have narrowly fallen short, you should think carefully before turning away from veterinary science, if that is really what you want to do. There are plenty of cases of people who have persisted and gained the extra practical experience that was needed to tip the scales in their favour. Determination to succeed is a quality that is generally recognised and supported. Think carefully before turning away to take another science subject. In most cases such a move will prove to be a decisive career choice. This is because it is not possible to transfer from another science course into veterinary school. Nor is it easy to take veterinary science as a second bachelor's degree: graduate applicants have to face stiffer competition and the prospect of having to pay high fees if accepted.

Retaking A levels

Many unsuccessful candidates decide to do a repeat year and take their examinations again. Before doing this it would be sensible to seek the advice of an admissions tutor. The fact is that not many people doing repeats are made conditional offers unless there are documented extenuating circumstances, such as serious illness. If you are made an offer it will usually be based upon the second attempt and the requirement will probably be raised to achieving grade A in all three subjects. You may get a repeat offer if you have narrowly failed to secure a place on the first try and are excellent in all other respects. However, most candidates who reapply have to take their chance in Clearing after a preliminary rejection.

The truth is that the almost overwhelming pressure of demand by highly motivated and well-qualified candidates is taking its toll on the chances of those repeating A levels. Selection is becoming more stringent, resulting in fewer re-sitters being successful.

It is possible to improve A level grades by retaking anything between one and six units, depending on how many times the units have been sat and how close you are to the A grade boundary. It is often sensible to retake AS units as they are easier than the A2 units. To achieve an A grade at A level you need to score 480 Uniform Mark Scale (UMS) marks out of 600, and it does not matter how the 480 is achieved, so it makes sense to gain as many of the 'easier' marks as possible. Your retake strategy will depend on how many extra marks you need and which examination board set your papers (which will determine when re-sits are available). Sixth-form colleges are usually happy to advise students about their options.

Case study

Having narrowly missed out on his A level grades, 19-year-old Joshua is currently studying to re-sit two of his subjects in January. Despite seeing all his friends go to university, Joshua has not been deterred and instead of seeing it as a setback, he has taken it as an opportunity.

Unconcerned as to the geographical locations of the veterinary schools, Joshua has made his choices based on the universities' specific work experience requirements.

His father is a doctor and his mother also works in the same profession, so Joshua has grown up surrounded by medical language. However, while interested in the human physique, it was the diversity of the animal kingdom that drew Joshua's focus.

'I have always liked animals since I went to a petting zoo at the age of four, and in many ways, I think that I have always known that I wanted to be a vet. Despite living in London, I was lucky enough to grow up in the valleys of Wales where my father still works. On many occasions, I helped our local farmers with the sheep on the hills, feeding them, shearing them and also with the lambing. Knowing exactly what I wanted to do with my life I applied for work experience in a variety of different places, both internationally and on the home front, and was even lucky enough to work at the RSPCA Harmsworth Memorial Hospital under the excellent tutelage of David Grant.

'I know that everyone claims this but I genuinely have always tried hard at my academics even though I do not naturally find them easy. I did not apply last year and I am grateful that I did not as I narrowly missed the required grades. Aside from anything else though, I wanted to gain as much experience as possible. Re-sitting my exams has been the best possible way forward for me as I feel more grounded now, even three months on.'

Providing that you meet the requirements of the specific university – both academically and practically – you should not feel disadvantaged from applying. It is worth remembering that there is a shortage of vets at the moment: however, that does not mean they take just anyone!

7 | So why did the chicken cross the road?
The interview

When the veterinary schools have received the UCAS applications, they will sift through them and decide who to call for interview. Only approximately one in three applicants to each institution will get an interview, but this can vary from year to year and between universities.

Timing

The timing of interviews can be anything from November to March, so some candidates have to wait some time before getting their interview, and because of this timescale some candidates will get a late decision. The Cambridge colleges usually conduct their interviews in December, along with those for other courses at the university.

The purpose of the interview

The interview is designed to find out more about you. In particular, the interviewers (possibly a panel) will want to satisfy themselves about your motivation and the extent of your commitment to becoming a qualified veterinary surgeon, and so they may ask you about the following areas.

- Have you an appropriate attitude towards animal welfare?
- Are you reasonably well informed about the implications of embarking on a veterinary career?
- Are you a mature person possessing a balanced outlook on life?
- Will they be satisfied that you have the ability to cope with the pace of what is generally acknowledged to be a long and demanding course?

To help them they will have your UCAS application, your referee's report and any supporting statements made by veterinary practitioners or people for whom you have worked. They will already have a good idea of your academic ability.

Preparation

Experience shows that personal qualities are just as important as academic ability, perhaps more so. The way you come across will be influenced by how confident you are. This does not mean being over-confident. Many people believe that they can get through interviews by thinking on their feet and taking each question as it comes. This is prob-ably an unwise attitude. Good preparation is the key. By being well informed on a variety of issues you will be able to formulate answers to most questions. There will always be the unexpected question for which no amount of preparation can help, but you can minimise the chance of this happening.

Confidence based on good preparation is the best kind. It is not the puffed-up variety that can soon be punctured by searching questions. While it is true that the interviewers will want to put you at your ease and will try to make the atmosphere informal and friendly, there is no doubt that for you there will be some tension in the situation. Think positively – this may be no bad thing. Many of us perform better when we are on our toes.

Some schools will be able to offer you a mock interview. Sometimes they can arrange for a person from outside the school to give the inter-view, which can help make it feel more realistic. If you are not sure about whether this facility is available, ask your school careers department. They will be keen to help if they can.

If you know anyone, student or staff, connected with one of the veteri-nary schools, ask for their advice. They may be able to give you an idea of what to expect. Start your preparation by looking at your copy of the personal statement you submitted to UCAS. This is the most important part of your UCAS application and it should tell the interviewers a lot about you as a person, your work experience, your interests and skills. Many of the questions they ask will be prompted by what you have writ-ten in it. The questions will most likely begin with those designed to put you at your ease. As the interview proceeds you should expect them to become more searching. Try practising your answers to questions like those shown below:

Question: *Did you have any trouble getting here?*

Comment: This is the sort of friendly question that is meant to get you started. Do not spend too long on it, but take the opportunity to be sociable, try to relax; and smile.

Question: *Have you visited here before?*

Comment: Did you go to the open day? If so, this is the moment to mention the fact. The interviewer will almost certainly follow up and ask what you thought of it. The faculty probably invested a lot of time and work in preparing it, so go easy on criticism! However, you should be prepared to say what you found was helpful and informative. It is then easier to make an additional constructive criticism. Bear in mind that the interviewers will expect you to have done your homework. If you hope to spend the next five or six years of your life at that institution, you should certainly have made efforts to see whether it is the right place for you. Although your choice is limited to four out of seven veterinary schools, you still have a choice to make. If you answer, 'No, but I've heard that you have a good reputation', you are hardly likely to convince them that you really want to go there. Similarly, answering, 'No, but I think that all of the veterinary schools are pretty similar' will not enhance your chances.

Question: *What did you think of our brochure?*

Comment: This is an alternative opening question on which you may have an opinion. Some veterinary schools, such as London, have their own brochure; others have entries in the main prospectus. Be prepared, show that you have at least read it and have an opinion. You could say, 'I thought that it was very informative about the structure of the course, and I particularly liked the case histories of your students – they made me realise that students in a similar situation to me can get a place.' Hopefully, this will lead to a question which will allow you to talk about your experience.

Question: *How do you think you are doing with your A levels?*

Comment: This is not a time for modesty. You would not be having this interview if your school had not predicted you will get good results. You should be sounding optimistic while at the same time indicating that you are working hard. They may also be interested to learn what are your favourite subjects so be ready for a follow-up question along those lines. If you have a good set of AS results, you could mention them at this point. You could also talk about a biology project which was relevant to veterinary science. As with the two previous examples, your aim should be to steer these rather boring questions towards topics that you have prepared and which will show you in the strongest light.

Question: *What do you think of the TV programmes about vets?*

Comment: Nowadays, programmes specifically about vets in the UK are seen as less marketable than programmes such as those documenting wildlife abroad or those featuring celebrities such as the late Steve Irwin: human nature is such that people are more interested by the exotic or the unknown. A few years ago there were several programmes on television following the everyday work of a vet. Such programmes were not always good for the professional standing of the vet. They made entertaining television, especially when they showed the animals and the caring 'honest broker' role of the vet between animals and humankind. They also almost universally presented vets as amiable people. On the other hand, though, you could argue that veterinary science was undermined when the programmes degenerated into 'soaps', with a portrayal of young vets whose work was an easy or incidental part of their lives. In your answer show that you have thought about television's influence.

Question: *Why do you want to study veterinary science?*

Comment: The direction of the interview can change quite suddenly. Be ready for the switch in questioning; the answer will bring into focus your attitude to animals, the range of your work experience, those important manual skills, and your commitment to all the hard work entailed in studying to become a qualified professional veterinary surgeon admitted to the Register of the RCVS. This is your opportunity, if you have not already done so, to mention your work experience, and to emphasise how your determination to become a vet increased as a result. This is an important question and needs a full answer, but keep your reply to under two minutes. Practise this. Remember that research findings show that if you exceed two minutes you risk boring your listeners.

Question: *Why do you want to come to this veterinary school?*

Comment: This is a natural follow-up question, so be prepared for it. The answer is personal to you: you may want to go to a new area of the country; you may know the area well because you have relations living there; your local vet may have recommended this particular veterinary school to you; the reputation of the school may have impressed you because of some particular speciality in which you are also interested. There could be several reasons, but make sure you give an honest answer; not just what you think the interviewer wants to hear.

Question: *Tell us something about your work experience with animals.*

Comment: This is one of the big questions of the interview. It would be surprising if the interviewers do not already have feedback from where you have been working. The interviewers will know what happens in a veterinary practice or on a farm, so lists of things that you saw or did will not shed any light on your suitability for the profession. Instead, concentrate on your reactions to the experience. Did you enjoy it? Were there any interesting or unusual cases that stick in your memory? Is your enthusiasm clear? Do you show your respect and sympathy for the animals? And what about the people – did you get on with them? The key phrases here are, 'For example, when I . . .' and 'For instance, I was able to . . .'

Question: *What are the main things you learned from your work experience?*

Comment: This is the typical follow-up question that gives you a chance to summarise and underline your impressions. You could try to indicate the varied nature of your experience, the different types of practice or farms you saw. There is also the business side of working with animals for which you may not originally have been prepared. Maybe you were astonished at the responsibilities of the veterinary nurses. Be prepared to intrigue your listeners. A related question is, 'From your work experience, what do you think are the qualities necessary to be a successful vet?'

Rather than answering, 'Stamina, communication, physical fitness, problem-solving . . .' and so on, bring in examples of things that you saw. For example: 'The ability to solve problems. For instance, when I accompanied a vet to a riding school, it was clear that one of the horses was very distressed, but it was unclear why . . .' and then go on to explain the steps involved in the diagnosis and treatment.

Question: *Have you ever felt frightened of animals?*

Comment: Vets shouldn't be frightened of animals, particularly small ones! However, honesty compels most of us to admit that we have at times and in certain situations felt vulnerable to a kick or bite. Explain the situation and what was said at the time – vets are noted for their humour!

Question: *What do you think of rearing animals for meat?*

Comment: This type of question might be asked because it checks on your motivation. Perhaps you should start by looking at it from the animal's viewpoint. Animals should be kept well with good standards of husbandry and eventually slaughtered humanely. Of course, the animal does not know the reason for its being slaughtered, but you do. Some of your future clients may be farmers who make their living from supplying meat or poultry – what is your reaction? If you oppose eating meat, you should be honest but make it clear that you would be able to remain professional.

Question: *How do you feel about cruelty to animals?*

Comment: With the strong interest in and liking for animals that you would expect from all veterinary students, they will be watching your reaction. This is a question that you should expect and your response, while putting animal welfare first, should be strong and well reasoned rather than too emotional. What would you do if you thought a farmer was acting in a cruel way to some of his livestock? Go to the police straight away? Talk over the difficulty with a colleague? Threaten the farmer by mentioning that you might bring in the RSPCA? The interviewers are not expecting you to come up with a perfect answer but rather to show that you are capable of coming up with a well-balanced and reasoned solution.

Remember: good preparation is the key.

Topical and controversial issues

Most interviews last only 15–20 minutes, so there may not be time for questions of a more topical or controversial nature. Nevertheless, it may be worth investing a little thought into how you might sketch out an answer to questions covering one or more of the following issues, each of which will be outlined in the next chapter:

- avian influenza (bird flu)
- bluetongue disease
- canine influenza
- methicillin-resistant Staphylococcus aureus (MRSA)
- bovine tuberculosis and badgers
- foot-and-mouth disease
- bovine spongiform encephalopathy (BSE)
- animal obesity
- swine influenza virus
- intensive farming
- fox hunting
- fall of dairy prices
- Dangerous Dogs Act
- hybrid dogs
- animal testing.

Remember, most of the time there is no right or wrong answer for questions relating to issues such as these. It is really a case of demonstrating your understanding of an issue, your quality of judgement and your ability to discuss the issue clearly, logically and succinctly. A burst of enthusiasm and conviction won't do any harm either.

Importance of the interview

These are just a few of the possible questions and issues that you might expect to come up at a selection interview for entry to veterinary school. To be called for interview is a positive sign as it indicates that your application is being considered and a good interview can lead to an offer. Another reason for trying to do well at the interview stage is that those candidates whose grades fall just below those required in their conditional offers are often reconsidered. If places are available, a good interview performance could tip the balance in your favour.

Demeanour

Most candidates will do their best to prepare well for the interview by anticipating likely questions. However, very few candidates realise that the visual impression they are creating will count for as much as their verbal answers to questions. It is a bit like the old saying, 'It's not what you say it's the way that you say it.'

Admissions tutors are unlikely to admit that they are going to be influenced by appearance and body language, but they are only human. There is bound to be subjectivity involved. What can you do about it? Try to look your best and try to be as relaxed as possible in what will seem to be a fairly tense situation. Here are a few points to watch.

Body language

When you first enter the room, smile and give a firm handshake. Veterinary schools are friendly places and like to exude informality. Sit comfortably and reasonably upright, leaning forward slightly. This position makes you look and feel alert. Try not to be so tense that you are crouching forward, giving an impression of a panther about to spring. Do not go to the other extreme of leaning back and looking irritatingly self-assured. Where do you put your hands during the interview? Try resting one on top of the other on your lap. Alternatively, let each hand rest by your side. It is not a good idea to have your arms folded – it looks as though you are shutting the interviewer out.

Speak clearly and deliberately. Do not rush things. When people are nervous they tend to speed up, which makes it harder for the listener. Make eye contact – looking at the person who asked you the question. If it is a panel interview, let your glance take in others at the table, make them feel that they are included. You should certainly have at least one mock interview, which, if possible, should be recorded on video so that you can see how you come across. You will then be able to spot any mannerisms, such as touching your head or cracking your knuckles, that might distract the interviewers.

Your appearance

Look your best. This does not mean that you should look like a tailor's dummy, but you should wear clothes which are smart, not showy, and in which you feel comfortable. Pay attention to details such as polishing your shoes and washing your hair.

Other issues

In addition to the topics listed above, it is advisable for an aspiring vet to have some prior knowledge of other issues that have affected the profession over the past decade. The most important of these are listed below. You are also strongly advised to check out the Defra website and look at some of the other global issues affecting animals today, such as African horse sickness, Koi herpes virus and West Nile virus.

Case study

'Most students who apply to become vets worry more about the interview than about the UCAS application, but what they should realise is that once you get to the interview stage you have a very good chance of being offered a place.'

So says Peter, who has just started his first year at Bristol, and received two offers when he applied. Peter took lots of advice from veterinary students and practising vets beforehand, many of whom emphasised that the interview was far less stressful than applicants imagine.

Peter went into the interview feeling nervous but also reasonably confident that he would be offered a place: 'I wasn't being arrogant in thinking I would get a place – it was because I had done lots of preparation. I knew that my work experience would probably be the main feature of the interview and I had kept a diary of all the things I had done and had seen. During my work experience I pestered the farmers and vets all the time with questions and at the end of each day I wrote down what they had said. I felt pretty sure that I could show the interviewers that I was genuinely interested in veterinary medicine.

'Before the interviews, I revised from my diaries in the same way I would revise for an exam. I also had some practice interviews with my school. At my real interviews, I was asked some general questions about the qualities a vet needs and I made sure I always illustrated these with examples of things I had actually seen or spoken about with the vets I worked with. In some ways I was over-prepared because I knew that only a fraction of what I had prepared would come up, but that also meant that I felt confident when I went into the interview.

'One of my friends was rejected and the feedback that he got after the interview (our school telephoned the vet school to find out why he had been rejected) was that he did not seem sufficiently interested in what he had encountered in his work experience – so I was extremely glad that I had prepared properly. In both interviews, the people there were friendly and helpful, encouraging me and they seemed to be interested in what I said. The time passed very quickly, though, and I was glad I was able to bring in my work experience very early in the interview.'

8 | Don't be an ostrich
Recent and current issues

It goes without saying that the more informed you are, the more realistic your chance of entering this profession, so keeping up to date with recent developments affecting the veterinary profession is not only important but compulsory. The best sources of information are the broadsheet newspapers and internet news websites such as that of the British Veterinary Association (BVA: www.bva.co.uk). As well as the news sections, the health sections contain articles that will be of interest. Your interviewer will want to find out whether you are genuinely interested in the profession, and alongside work experience, this includes testing your knowledge, awareness and appreciation of important issues: after all, if you are planning to devote the next 40 or so years of your life to veterinary science, you ought to be interested in issues that affect the profession.

Read a newspaper every day, cut out or photocopy articles of interest, and keep them in a scrapbook so that you can revise from them before your interview. You will also find the Defra website (www.defra.gov.uk) extremely helpful. Other useful websites are listed in Chapter 10.

At the time of going to print, the issues below are all listed by the BVA as being the most important current topics affecting the industry. In an interview the issue isn't necessarily about providing the right answers to questions but rather it is about having a depth of knowledge from which you can open a discussion and show the clarity of analytical thought needed to be a vet. In many ways it is symptomatic of the profession and therefore good preparation. Good research ahead of your interview will also give you the confidence to feel able to discuss these issues with a professional.

Avian influenza (bird flu)

The first human case of Avian flu or bird flu was in Hong Kong in 1997. Before then it wasn't known that this type of illness could be passed from birds directly to humans. The virus is spread when infected birds excrete the virus in their faeces. Once this dries it becomes a powder and is therefore easily inhaled. Symptoms are similar to other types of flu – fever, malaise, sore throat and coughing. People can also develop conjunctivitis. All 18 people infected in 1997 had been in close contact with live birds in markets or on farms.

Countries known to have been affected by the disease include Cambodia, Indonesia, South Korea, China, Japan, Thailand, Vietnam and Hong Kong. Furthermore, since January 2004, human cases of avian influenza have been reported in Asia, Africa, the Pacific region and Europe. Avian flu has been seen to have a high fatality rate in humans. In 1997, six out of the 18 people who were infected died. In an outbreak in 2004, there were over 20 confirmed deaths.

There are 15 different strains of the virus; it is the H5N1 strain which is infecting humans and causing high death rates. Even within the H5N1 strain, however, variations are seen, and slightly different strains are being seen in the different countries where there have been outbreaks of the disease. The H5N1 virus that emerged in Asia in 2003 continues to evolve and may adapt so that other mammals may be susceptible to infection as well. Moreover, it is likely that H5N1 infection among birds has become endemic in certain areas and that human infections resulting from direct contact with infected poultry and/or wild birds will continue to occur. So far, the spread of the H5N1 virus from person to person has been rare and limited.

Patients suffering from avian flu are being treated with antiviral drugs while researchers continue to work to develop a vaccine. In 2004, the EU announced that it was considering a precautionary ban on the importation of poultry meat and products from Thailand. At the same time, millions of birds were culled in an attempt to stop the spread of the disease among birds, which would in turn prevent it being passed on to humans. Currently, there is a ban on the importation of birds and bird products from H5N1-affected countries. The regulation states that no person may import or attempt to import any birds, whether dead or alive, or any products derived from birds (including hatching eggs), from the specified countries.

In January 2006, two children from the eastern Turkish town of Dogubeyazit, whose family kept poultry at their home, died having contracted the virulent H5N1 strain. Three months later, in the Scottish town of Fife, tests confirmed that a swan there had died from the deadly H5N1 strain of the avian flu virus. The discovery made Britain the 14th country in Europe to have the disease in its territory.

The first major outbreak in the UK was in February 2007, on a turkey farm in Suffolk. There have been further such instances, the latest one being in Oxfordshire where the highly pathogenic H7N7 strain – a subtype of the species influenza A virus – was found in laying hens. In November 2008 the UK became free from Avian influenza as defined by the rules of the World Organisation for Animal Health (OIE).

Bluetongue disease

Bluetongue, which has now been downgraded by Defra in level of severity, is an insect-borne viral disease to which all species of ruminants are susceptible, although sheep are most severely affected. It is characterised by changes to the mucous linings of the mouth and nose and the coronary band of the foot. It was first described in South Africa but has since been recognised in most countries in the tropics and sub-tropics. Since 1999, there have been widespread outbreaks in Greece, Italy, Corsica and the Balearic Islands. Cases have also occurred in Bulgaria, Croatia, Macedonia and Serbia. It appears that the virus has spread from both Turkey and north Africa. One possible reason for the changing pattern of bluetongue disease in the Mediterranean region is climate changes. Further changes could lead to the disease spreading northward. In September 2007, the first suspected UK case was reported in a Highland cow in Ipswich, Suffolk. Since then the virus has spread from cattle to sheep in Britain.

The clinical signs can vary from unapparent to mild or severe, depending on the virus strain and the breed of sheep involved. Deaths of sheep in a flock can be as high as 70%. Animals that survive the disease will lose condition with a reduction in meat and wool production.

Bluetongue has been found in Australia, the USA, Africa, the Middle East and other parts of Asia and in Europe – with cases reported in the Netherlands, Belgium, parts of western Germany and areas of northern France. In order to control the infection, a protection zone boundary of 20km is set up to control the movement of animals and a further surveil-lance zone of 150km is put in place to monitor for any signs of the dis-ease spreading. In the restriction zone, rules apply to movement of ruminants, export of animals is prohibited and all animals on premises within this zone have to be identified and checked for bluetongue.

Two years ago, Bluetongue Serotype 6 (BTV6) was confirmed on three farms in the Netherlands and, as a result, on 20 October 2008 all exports from the Netherlands to other EU member states were banned as a precautionary measure while these cases are investigated. The ban is still in place.

There are no reports of transmission to humans.

Canine influenza

Canine influenza refers to a new strain of the influenza A virus that causes influenza in canines. It is a contagious respiratory disease that often has the same signs as kennel cough – sneezing, coughing and fever – and requires veterinary medical attention. The disease came to light at a Florida racetrack when greyhound fatalities from respiratory illnesses were attributed to a mutated strain of the deadly equine influenza virus (H3N8) that has been detected in horses for over 40 years. Dogs have no natural immunity to this virus owing to a lack of previous exposure and therefore transmission rates between canines are recorded as being very high. Having affected the majority of American states, this specific strain of the influenza virus has now reached endemic levels.

Statistically, roughly 100% of canines that come in contact with the virus – regardless of age or vaccination history – become infected. Of those infected, 20% show no signs of the virus. Of the 80% that exhibit signs, there have been two forms observed:

- mild infection – symptoms include a low fever, possible nasal discharge and a persistent cough that can last anything up to three weeks
- severe infection – symptoms include a high fever, increased respiratory rates, which leads to difficulty breathing, and potentially other indicators of pneumonia.

However, the more positive news is that research shows fatality in only 8% of infected canines, making it a disease with a high morbidity but a low mortality rate.

Canine influenza is believed to be a mainly airborne virus – i.e. transmitted by sneezing or coughing – with an affected dog able to spread the virus for seven to 10 days after contracting the strain. Symptoms will present within two to five days. It is also worth bearing in mind that infected dogs can spread the virus without exhibiting signs of disease in themselves.

Treatment of canine influenza will vary from case to case. Early symptoms may only require a course of antibiotics to stop any secondary bacterial infections but in more serious cases could require the same treatment that humans receive in influenza cases, i.e. fluids (supplied intravenously in severe cases) and rest. There is, as yet, no recognisable vaccine to prevent canine influenza, although investigation continues into a canarypox-vectored vaccine – used for treatment of equine influenza – for use in dogs.

Once again, the virus is not known to infect humans or poultry.

MRSA

Methicillin-resistant Staphylococcus aureus (MRSA) – or 'superbug' – is a major health concern very much in the news for causing outbreaks in hospitals around the UK. Primarily affecting humans, as the BVA says, it may also colonise and cause infection in companion and farm animals. MRSA is of little risk to healthy animals and although transmission of infection from animals to humans has been documented, the rate is thought to be low. The evidence available points to humans as the source of the MRSA strains.

Staphylococcus aureus is a bacterium, strains of which live harmlessly on the skin and in the nose of about a third of normal healthy people. The problem arises when it enters the body, and it thrives in hospitals among those who are more susceptible due to the nature of their illnesses weakening their immune system. MRSA can often enter the body through cuts, grazes and wounds, whether accidental or deliberate, i.e. those made out of necessity for surgery.

Different strains of MRSA usually affect animals and humans. They are particularly adept at colonising and/or infecting their preferred host species. For example, the staphylococci that commonly infect and colonise dogs are usually from a different species, known as Staphylococcus intermedius, which differs in certain characteristics from Staphylococcus aureus. Although strains of the latter may have a preferred host species, they can opportunistically infect other species in some circumstances.

Reported cases of MRSA infection in animals can be traced back to 1999 and are often reported in the media, although there was an incident back in the mid-1980s regarding a cat resident in a rehabilitation ward for the elderly. Since then, dogs, cats, rabbits and horses have all been diagnosed with the MRSA infection. This problem is not isolated to the UK, but is seen throughout the world, with cases reported in the USA, Korea, Japan and Brazil. There is even evidence of pigs now being affected in the Netherlands.

There is no current evidence that suggests MRSA affects food-producing animals (i.e. farmed livestock) in the UK. Most MRSA infections, particularly in cats and dogs, have been post-operative infections, usually from wounds. The numbers of skin, ear, urinary tract and bronchial infections have been lower.

MRSA is a problem that will continue to trouble both humans and beasts, because the effectiveness of antibiotics is constantly being challenged by the virus developing resistance to the drug.

Bovine tuberculosis (bTB) and badgers

Bovine tuberculosis (bTB) is a serious disease in cattle. Although the risk of tuberculosis spreading to humans through milk or meat is slight, it can be transmitted through other means, particularly to farm workers who have direct contact with the animals. The number of cattle slaughtered because of bTB increased from 599 in 1986 to 22,570 in 2004. In 2008 the number was roughly 40,000 and in January to March 2009 there was a 20% rise on the same period in 2008. The National Farmers' Union has estimated that the cost in compensation to British farmers could easily reach £1 billion by 2013. There is uncertainty about the cause of the spread of bTB in cattle, but many people believe that it is passed on by badgers – a protected species. There is widespread support within the farming community for the culling of badgers, but this is opposed by wildlife and conservation groups. In 1998 the government set up a badger-culling trial as well as taking steps to test the carcasses of badgers killed on the roads (about 50,000 every year) in order to try to find out more about the causes of the disease in cattle. However, the results were inconclusive, and the two opposing sides in the argument are still at loggerheads: the fundamental question remains unanswered – is bTB spread from badgers to cattle, from cattle to badgers, or is other wildlife involved?

In November 2004 the government introduced enhanced testing and control measures to help improve the detection of bTB, so that action could be taken quickly to prevent the spread of the disease. A 10-year government strategic framework for the sustainable control of bTB in Great Britain was published in March 2005. Through this framework, the government aims to bring about a sustainable improvement in control of bTB by 2015. In December 2005, the government also announced pre-movement testing in England and Wales to help reduce the risk of bTB spreading between herds.

According to recent data, there was a reduction in the number of new bTB incidents in 2005 and again in 2006. Despite this reduction, however, levels of bTB remain high in comparison with other EU countries. On 7 July 2008, Hilary Benn MP, the then Secretary of State for Environment, Food and Rural Affairs, issued a statement to Parliament about bTB and badgers, which declared that government policy was that licences would not be issued to allow badger culling to control bTB for fear the cull might make things worse. He went on to say that £20 million would be invested in vaccinations for badgers and cattle over three years. Mr Benn also intimated that he wanted to work closely with the industry in order to find the appropriate solution and in conjunction with Defra, a bovine TB Partnership Group is to be established.

Foot-and-mouth disease

The outbreak of foot-and-mouth disease (FMD) that occurred in February 2001 was the first in the UK for 20 years. Between February and September, 2,030 cases occurred. The last major outbreak was in 1967, during which about half a million animals were slaughtered. Before the re-emergence of the disease, in a new and highly virulent form, it had been thought that FMD had been eradicated from western Europe. The latest form of the virus seems to have originated in Asia, and could have been brought into the UK in a number of ways. Something as trivial as a discarded sandwich containing meat from an infected source – brought into the country by, for example, a tourist – could have been incorporated into pigswill (pig feed made from waste food) and then passed on to animals from other farms at a livestock sale. The bovine spongiform encephalopathy (BSE) problem (see page 76) led to greater regulation of abattoirs, which resulted in the closure of many smaller abattoirs. Animals destined for slaughter now have to travel greater distances and the possibility of FMD being passed to other animals is, as a consequence, greater.

The UK was declared foot-and-mouth free on 14 January 2002, almost a year after the first reported case. More than four million animals, from over 7,000 farms, were slaughtered during this period. The last recorded case occurred at the end of September 2001. The official report highlighted the lack of speed with which the government acted and commented on the fact that the understaffed State Veterinary Service was unable to effectively monitor the disease. The disease took a month to diagnose and by the time animal movement was halted, over 20,000 infected sheep had spread the virus across the UK.

Defra states that:

> 'FMD is endemic in parts of Asia, Africa and South America, with sporadic outbreaks in disease-free areas. Countries affected by FMD recently include Afghanistan, Bhutan, Iran, Lebanon, Peru, South Africa, the United Arab Emirates and Vietnam.'
>
> www.defra.gov.org

There have been no outbreaks of the disease in the EU since the 2001 outbreak which affected not only the UK but also Ireland, France and the Netherlands.

A Royal Society report recommended that vaccination – commonly used in a number of countries – should be a weapon in any future outbreaks. Vaccination is unpopular with some meat exporters since it is difficult to distinguish between animals that have been vaccinated and those that have the disease, and for this reason many FMD-free countries ban the import of vaccinated cattle.

FMD is a viral disease that affects cattle, pigs, sheep, goats and deer. Hedgehogs and rats (and elephants!) can also become infected, and people, cats, dogs and game animals can carry infected material. The virus can be transferred by saliva, milk and dung; it can also become airborne and travel large distances, perhaps as far as 150 miles. A vehicle that has driven through dung from an infected animal can carry the virus to other farms on its tyres. FMD is more contagious than any other animal disease, and the mortality rate among young animals is high.

The role of the veterinary surgeon in a suspected outbreak of FMD is not a pleasant one. If the existence of the disease is confirmed, the vet must make arrangements with Defra to ensure that all animals on the farm (and possibly on neighbouring farms) are slaughtered and then incinerated. For economic reasons, there is no question of the vet being allowed to try to treat infected animals.

There has only been one recorded case of FMD in a human being in Great Britain and that was in 1966. The general effects of the disease in that case were similar to influenza, with some blisters. It is a mild, short-lived, self-limiting disease. The Food Standards Agency has advised that the disease in animals has no implications for the human food chain.

BSE

BSE – commonly referred to as mad cow disease – was first identified in 1986, although it is possible that it had been known about since 1983. It is a neurological disease that affects the brains of cattle, and is similar to scrapie, a disease of sheep that has been known about since the 18th century. In 1988, the government's working party, chaired by Sir Richard Southwood, stated that there was minimal risk to humans since, as scrapie was known not to spread to humans, neither would BSE. It is believed that BSE originated in cattle as a result of the practice of using the remains of diseased sheep as part of high-protein cattle feed in an attempt to increase milk yields. In 1989, the government recommended that specific offal – such as the brain and the spleen – should be discarded rather than allowed to enter the food chain, and that diseased cattle should be incinerated. In the early 1990s, the increased incidence of Creutzfeldt–Jakob disease (CJD) – a disease similar to BSE that affects humans – caused scientists to look at the possibility that the disease had jumped species. At about the same time, scientists found increasing evidence of transmission between species following experiments involving mice, pigs and cats. By 1993, there were over 800 new cases of BSE a week, despite the ban on animal feed containing specified offal. It became clear that the increase in the cases of CJD was related to the rise in BSE, and that it was likely that millions of infected cattle had been eaten before the symptoms appeared. In 1996, the EU banned the export of cattle, beef and beef products that originated in the UK. In 1997, the government set up a public inquiry, chaired by Lord Phillips. The findings were released in October 2000. Details can be found on the inquiry website (www.bseinquiry.gov.uk). The total number of confirmed cases of BSE in Great Britain since 1986 is estimated to be about 185,000.

There has been an overall decline in the epidemic in recent years, with confirmed cases now falling by around 50% each year.

The BSE problem raised a number of issues concerning farming and food safety. In retrospect, the decision to allow the remains of diseased animals to be incorporated into feed for herbivores seems to be misguided, at the very least. The problem with BSE is that the infecting agent, the prion (a previously unknown pathogen composed of proteins) was able to survive the treatments used to destroy bacteria and viruses. If any good has come out of the problem, it is that we are now much more aware of food safety. In April 2000, the government established the Food Standards Agency, created to 'protect public health from risks which may arise in connection with the consumption of food, and otherwise to protect the interests of consumers in relation to food'. Although it was established by the government, it can independently publish any advice that it gives the government, in order to avoid the accusations of cover-ups and secrecy levelled at the government over the BSE affair.

In March 2006, EU veterinary experts agreed unanimously to lift the ban on British beef exports, imposed 10 years earlier to prevent the spread of BSE. The EU's standing committee on the food chain and animal health said that the UK had fulfilled all the conditions for the ban to end. The closure of export markets had cost the British beef industry around £675 million.

Animal obesity

Researchers at the University of Glasgow have found that six out of 10 pet dogs are overweight or obese. Like humans, animals are putting on weight as a result of a number of factors, including being fed scraps from the dinner table, lack of exercise and even how old or rich their owners are.

According to the university's website:

> 'The study in the Journal of Small Animal Practice assessed the body condition of 696 dogs. Owners were asked how often they fed their dog, what type of food was given, how often the dog was exercised, and the owner's age and household income. The results showed that 35.3% of the dogs had an ideal body shape, 39% were overweight, and 20.4% were obese; a further 5.3% were underweight.'

Obesity can have a huge impact on the animal's health as it exacerbates a range of medical conditions, including arthritis, expiratory airway dysfunction and lifespan.

The income of the owners was also a factor:

> 'The dogs whose owners earned less than £10,000 a year were much more likely to be obese or overweight than those whose owners earned £40,000 or more.'

www.gla.ac.uk

Swine influenza virus

This is a very common occurrence in pig populations: about half of the USA's pigs are thought to have the virus. While the recent swine flu outbreak has made the news in terms of its effects on humans, transmission of the virus from pigs to humans is relatively uncommon and does not always lead to human influenza, resulting only in the production of antibodies in the blood. While it is uncommon, people with regular exposure to pigs are at increased risk of swine flu infection. If this causes human influenza, it is called zoonotic swine flu.

In pigs, three influenza A virus subtypes (H1N1, H1N2 and H3N2) are the most common strains worldwide. In the United States, the H1N1 subtype was exclusively prevalent among swine populations before 1998; however, since late August 1998, H3N2 subtypes have been isolated from pigs. As of 2004, H3N2 virus isolates in US swine and turkey stocks were triple reassortants, containing genes from human (HA, NA and PB1), swine (NS, NP and M), and avian (PB2 and PA) lineages.

Transmission of the influenza virus is between infected and unaffected animals, with close transport, intensive farming and airborne infection all reasons for the spread of infection. Wild boar are considered to spread the disease between farms. The symptoms are sneezing, coughing, lethargy, decreased appetite and difficulty breathing.

As swine influenza is rarely fatal to pigs, little effort is made to treat the infection, with efforts instead being focussed on stopping the spread of infection between farms. Antibiotics do exist, though, and are used to treat the symptoms of influenza.

Intensive farming

Meat and dairy products feature prominently in the British diet. Although carbohydrates (such as pasta and rice) comprise a greater proportion of our diet than they did 10 years ago, we still eat protein in higher quantities than is consumed by our southern European neighbours. We also demand cheap food. The meat, poultry, dairy and egg industries are faced with a choice – to use technological methods in order to keep the price of their products as low as possible, or to allow the animals that they farm to lead more 'natural' lives which would necessarily reduce yields and increase costs. The use of drugs, hormones and chemicals is almost universal in farming (except in the organic farming movement), as are methods to control the movement of livestock by the use of pens, cages or stalls.

The veterinary profession is faced with a number of difficult decisions. It has to balance the pressure to produce cheap food with its primary aim of maintaining and improving animal welfare. An example of this is the use of antibiotics. Antibiotics are used in farming to treat sick animals. However, they are also used to protect healthy animals against the diseases associated with intensive farming and as growth promoters. The Soil Association reports that about 1,225 tonnes of antibiotics are used each year in the UK, over 60% of which are used for farm animals or by vets. The problem with antibiotics is that bacteria become resistant to them, and overuse of antibiotics in animals has these serious effects:

- resistant strains of bacteria, such as salmonella and Escherichia coli, can be passed on to humans, causing illness and, in extreme cases, death
- bacteria can develop resistance to the drugs that are used to treat serious illness in humans.

Other issues that concern the veterinary profession include:

- the welfare of live farm animals that are exported for slaughter
- battery farming of poultry
- the use of growth hormones
- humane killing of farm animals in abattoirs.

The Protection of Animals Act (1911) contains the general law relating to the suffering of animals, and agricultural livestock is also protected by more recent legislation. New regulations, incorporating EU law, came into force in August 2000. The regulations cover laying hens, poultry, calves, cattle, pigs and rabbits. More specifically, the EU has banned the use of veal crates from 2007 and traditional battery cages from 2012. Details of the regulations can be found on the Defra website (www.defra.gov.uk).

Fox hunting

While not necessarily an issue concerning vets, it is certainly something that you should have an appreciation of as it does concern the animal world. Most people have a view on the issue of hunting with hounds. Prior to the Hunting Act of 2004, there were those, on the one hand, who argued that fox hunting was an integral part of rural life, a country-side tradition; that foxes kill farm animals and therefore need to be controlled, that thousands of rural jobs would be lost if it were banned and that a ban on fox hunting would lead to a ban on other pastimes, such as shooting and fishing. On the other hand, many people believe that it was a cruel and unnecessary way to control foxes, claiming that around 20,000 foxes were killed every year and that about half that number of hunting dogs were also killed taking part in the sport. Animal rights activists believed it was immoral to chase and kill animals for sport.

The Hunting Act of 2004, which banned fox hunting in England and Wales, took effect in February 2005. The Act makes it an offence to hunt a wild mammal with a dog. Nevertheless, some forms of hunting are exempt, including those using no more than two dogs to flush out a mammal to be shot. Controversy on what is a very emotive subject therefore still remains. On the first anniversary of the ban, in February 2006, hunt supporters called for the Act to be repealed while the League Against Cruel Sports accused 33 hunts of repeatedly breaching the law.

For opposing sides of an argument which continues to be pursued, you should investigate the websites hosted by the League Against Cruel Sports (www.league.uk.com) and the Countryside Alliance (www.countryside-alliance.org).

Fall in dairy prices

The UK is the ninth largest milk producer in the world and the third largest in Europe. Although largely (90%) self-sufficient in milk, the UK participates in a significant trade in milk production. Nevertheless, farmers' unions are warning that the UK dairy industry is facing meltdown unless a national dairy body is established that can regulate farm gate milk prices.

Milk prices have been low for a number of years and this has been reflected in dairy farm incomes. Prices are expected to fall further as a result of the reform of the Common Agricultural Policy (CAP). Of additional concern to farmers is the fact that some sectors of the supply chain, for example supermarkets, are earning far greater profits than others. As a consequence, some dairy farmers are leaving the industry.

The Dairy Supply Chain Forum is working hard to understand why these farmers are leaving. While it is likely that profitability is an important factor, there are also issues such as succession of ownership and possibilities for diversification which need to be considered.

In an open letter to the Prime Minister, in September 2006, one farm business consultant, David Hughes, referred to the plight of UK dairy farmers as follows.

> 'Today UK milk producers receive approximately 10 pence per pint for milk that costs 11.5 pence per pint to produce. The same milk retails for at least 27 pence per pint in the major supermarkets or up to 48 pence per pint on the doorstep. Production costs have been pared to the bone and there is little or nothing that family farms can do to achieve further savings. Put simply, the balance of power within the supply chain is weighted entirely in favour of the large retailers, with a relatively weak processing sector competing to meet their demands. The individual milk producer has no bargaining power at all. If society chooses to ignore this gross imbalance of power we will rapidly witness the demise of the family-run dairy farm. They will be replaced by a small number of industrial milk factories that will contribute nothing to our countryside. Worse still, we could end up importing our entire milk supply with all the attendant strategic risks and environmental damage caused by increased food miles.'

Dangerous Dogs Act

The Dangerous Dogs Act, which was introduced in 1991, banned the ownership, breeding, sale and exchange and advertising for sale of specified types of fighting dogs. The dogs covered by the ban included the pit bull terrier. The Act was amended in 1997, one of the effects of which was to lift the mandatory destruction orders that courts applied to dogs found to be of those types listed in the Act. It is now possible, therefore, for prohibited dogs to be added to the Index of Exempted Dogs, but only at the direction of a court and only if the necessary conditions are met (tattooing, microchipping, etc.). No owner may apply to have their dog added to the index – it is entirely a matter for the courts to decide upon. The maximum penalty for illegal possession of a prohibited dog is a fine of £5,000 and/or six months' imprisonment.

Should this issue arise at interview, it is important to demonstrate that you are aware that vicious attacks by certain breeds of unmuzzled dogs on children and adults led to the Act requiring owners to register such dogs with the police and to keep them muzzled. For the qualified vet, controversy might arise if they are called on to destroy, for example, an unmuzzled pit bull terrier before it has committed an offence.

Is such action contrary to the professional oath of a veterinary surgeon? (Privately, many vets say that the Act is unworkable.) If you take a view on this in an interview you will get credit for at least knowing about the law, whether the interviewer agrees with your conclusion or not.

Hybrid dogs

In a consumer-focused society, designer dogs have become the new fad. But does this pose any danger? From Labradoodles to Puggles, dogs are turning into handbag accessories rather than family pets or functional animals. Originally these designer dogs were designed as a hypo-allergenic version of the guide dog but the issue of hybrid breeds throws up an ethical question. Hybrid dogs are now sold for staggering amounts of money, and it does ask questions of what hope is there for the adoption of other dogs and for rescue shelters. However, the advantage of breeding 'designer' or hybrid dogs can often be a reduction in the level of genetic defects or health problems found in particular breeds of pedigree dog. The hybrid dog has a much larger genetic pool and therefore a lower risk of suffering from the same health problems of either one of its parents. Hybrid dog-breeding remains a controversial topic but one which you should know about and be happy to comment on in terms of both advantages and disadvantages.

Animal testing

Almost all of the drugs used to treat people have been tested on animals. Without rigorous and controlled testing there are significant health risks associated with the use of new medicines. In many cases, the long-term or side effects of drugs can be more serious than the illness itself, and testing is therefore essential. Lord Winston, who pioneered in vitro fertilisation (IVF) and who found wider publicity through his BBC television series *The Human Body*, in response to a report by the Lords Select Committee on Science and Technology, was quoted in the *Independent* as saying: 'Perceived pressure may persuade people to go down a route which is not going to promote human welfare. We have a major job – animal research is essential for human welfare. Every drug we use is based on it. Without it those drugs would be unsafe.'

Each year British laboratories experiment on approximately three million animals. British law requires that any new drug must be tested on at least two different species of live mammal, one of which must be a large non-rodent. UK regulations are considered some of the most rigorous in the world – the Animals Act of 1986 insists that no animal experiments be conducted if there is a realistic alternative.

The debate on animal testing has become a high-profile one because of the activities of animal rights groups. Although the majority of animal rights groups campaign peacefully, the newspapers have given a good deal of publicity to a number of attacks on research laboratories. Huntingdon Life Sciences (HLS), a 50-year-old product development company, has been at the forefront of recent controversy over animal testing. The company claims that it works with a variety of resources, including pharmaceuticals and veterinary products, to help its manufacturers develop safer goods for the market. Some of its opponents claim that HLS kills 500 animals a day in tests for products such as weed killer, food colourings and drugs. In April 2003, HLS won a High Court injunction preventing protesters going within 50 yards of the homes of staff. In the same month activists held protests at three colleges of Cambridge University against the proposal for a primate experimentation laboratory at Girton College. Oxford University, like HLS, sought to obtain an injunction against animal rights protesters following opposition to a new research laboratory. Like HLS, Oxford was also successful. Protests and demonstrations, however, concerning these cases and other cases of animal testing, continue to this day.

Opposition to animal testing is centred on the idea that if animals are similar enough to us for test results to be meaningful, then they are too similar to be experimented upon. Conversely, drugs tested on animals have also gone on to have devastating effects on humans. Examples are the drug thalidomide and the drug trial in March 2006 which caused six men to have multiple organ failure. Campaigners argue that there are alternative methods of testing that do not involve animals. Many of these methods are, they say, also cheaper, quicker and more effective. They include:

- culture of human cells – this is already used in research into cancer, Parkinson's disease and acquired immune deficiency syndrome (AIDS)

- molecular methods, including DNA analysis
- use of micro-organisms
- computer modelling
- use of human volunteers.

Case study

Katherine applied to study veterinary medicine/science last year, and received one offer. She is now in her first year at Nottingham. Katherine was worried about the level of interest in veterinary-related issues required for an interview. 'Some people say to read as much as possible in order to have plenty to talk about in the interview; however, you should not try to be too scientific in your answers – after all, you are going to university to study veterinary medicine! Knowing about the practical aspects of being a vet was far more helpful in an interview.

'Therefore do your research. There are a lot of topical issues of late, swine influenza being the most obvious topic. You won't be able to know everything about every new issue, change in the law, or treatment, but have a reasonable knowledge about the topics in general. In my interview, I was asked a question about the spread of infectious diseases amongst farm animals and so I was able to use what I had learned about swine influenza as an example. Talking with professionals was the best way to understand things and working in a vet's surgery meant that I could ask questions about the profession. This was much more helpful to me than trying to read about these things because if I didn't understand something I was able to ask him.

'It is still the case that the law or government guidelines for farmers change quickly. This is a constant source of complaint amongst the farmers vets deal with so at least I have an under-standing of this now, which has given me an insight into veteri-nary science in a different sense. It's always a good idea to have thought about the negatives to the profession as well and to have discussed those with a professional, as this shows that you have thought about this.'

9 | Snakes and ladders
Career paths

There may be hidden expenses in training to be a vet but at least you can reflect, with some optimism, that a degree in veterinary science is going to result in a professional qualification and a job. According to figures published in the Royal College of Veterinary Surgeons (RCVS) Annual Report 2010, over 82% of registered surgeons were in practice and roughly 73% of those are in the UK (bear in mind that these figures only reflect those surgeons registered with the RCVS on 31 March 2010). However, there is currently a real shortage of vets. A glance through the pages of the *Veterinary Record* will confirm the strong demand for the newly qualified vet to go into practice. Indeed, a report on the BBC's Donal MacIntyre programme back in May 2008 revealed that pets' lives are actually at risk because of a shortage of fully qualified veterinary staff. While the 16,000 practising UK vets employ veterinary nurses, only 7,500 veterinary nurses are actually qualified. In September 2008, the RCVS welcomed the input of the Migration Advisory Committee (MAC) and its recommendations to the government regarding the lack of skilled workers in the UK. So while it is now up to the government to act accordingly, the veterinary profession has been listed by the Home Office as a Skills Shortage Occupation for many years now. To put the vets shortage in the UK in perspective, 55% of new registrations to the RCVS of the past five years have been from overseas applicants, which is an average of 702 each year.

Professional Development Phase (PDP)

Once you have graduated from your veterinary degree course, you are still not there yet. The year after graduation is known as the Professional Development Phase (PDP), during which you will be expected to develop your skills. The RCVS has developed a set of Year One Competencies so that you can record your progress. After that you will always be expected to keep up with your continuing professional development (CPD) by attending courses and lectures and networking. Once you have qualified, you might wish to consider working in the types of practice or roles described in this chapter.

Career opportunities

The universities' first destination statistics show that nearly all graduates begin their careers in practice, but such is the variety of opportunity in this profession that career change and divergence can and does occur. Graduates are employed in the government service dealing with investigation, control and eradication of diseases. There are also opportunities for veterinary scientists to become engaged in university teaching and research establishments at home and abroad.

If you start in general practice, there is the chance to move into different types of practice. The trend is towards small-animal practices. There is also more opportunity to work with horses – now seen as an important part of the growing leisure industry. There is also a growing trend towards specialisation within practices. Areas of specialisation include cattle, horses, household pets and even exotics. Specialisation can also be more sophisticated – for example combining equine care with lameness in all animals. Dermatology, soft tissues and cardiology are examples of the kinds of specialisation which are seen as helpful to clients. It is possible for postgraduate specialist qualifications to be obtained through the RCVS's specialist certificate and diploma examinations.

Veterinary variety – types of vet

As your degree progresses, you will most likely find an area of veterinary medicine that you particularly enjoy or have a certain flair for. Before you reach that stage, though, it is worthwhile considering which course immediately strikes you as something to which you feel you could dedicate the next 40 years of your working life. However, it is highly advisable to start your career in general practice, working with household animals or even with larger animals on a farm, before you specialise in one of the more diverse forms of veterinary surgery.

Small-animal vet

The RCVS Manpower Survey in 2006 revealed that 72% of a vet's time is spent with small animals. The most common type of vet, a small-animal vet, works in local practice and deals with the care and treatment of household pets. You will be concerned with anything from vaccinations to neutering, as well as local surgery and general health check-ups. In unfortunate situations, you may be required to make the decision as to the kindness of putting an animal down to ease its pain.

Large-animal vet

Principally concerned with multiple animals in a group as opposed to individual animals, a large-animal vet is most often found on a farm, and is concerned with the health and productivity of the herd. Your responsibilities are likely to involve the treatment of disease and giving advice on the husbandry of the animals, including nutritional balance and sanitation. This role requires a strong will and a thick skin when dealing with farmers, who are an entirely different clientele to the ordinary public. Once you have the respect and confidence of the farmer, your job will be far easier.

Equine vet

As the name suggests, equine vets specialise in the treatment of horses. Stable and horse owners alike prefer to use a specialist equine vet when it comes to the treatment of their animals because horses are different from other animals in all respects – from anatomy to pharmacology. Horses also require different husbandry and therefore as a specialist you will be giving a different form of advice. Before specialising in this area, it is essential, or at least highly advisable, that you train in general practice as a smaller-animal vet and then progress to achieving your specialist qualifications later on once you have general experience to your name.

Exotic-animal vet

Exotic-animal vets have specialist training in the treatment of exotic animals including snakes and turtles. The term 'exotic' is wide-ranging, and it is worth remembering that ferrets and small rodents are included in this category. As with an equine vet, becoming a general vet first is a prerequisite before taking your specialist qualifications. There is an element of glamour in this work and you can expect to find yourself spending a lot of time at a zoo working with wild animals.

Avian vet

Avian vets are concerned with the treatment of birds and this specialisation offers you a diverse working environment. One day might be spent in private practice, the next in a bird sanctuary and the next in a zoo. You would certainly never be bored! The same advice applies as above: you should take prior work in general practice before specialising with the requisite qualifications – as working with smaller animals will help you appreciate the smaller anatomical size of a bird.

Other types of vet

The vets listed above are the most common types of veterinary surgeons in the UK. However, this list is by no means comprehensive and should you wish to, you can also specialise in the following areas:

- cardiology (work based on the study of an animal's heart)
- dental (mouth-based work, including teeth, gums and hygiene)
- feline (working with cats, large and small – can expect zoo-based work)
- holistic (emphasises the study of all aspects of an animal's health, including physical, psychological, social, economic and cultural factors)
- marine (caring for marine-based animals such as dolphins and whales – strong swimming ability is a prerequisite).

The veterinary practice

There are many different types of veterinary practice. The majority, however, deal with all species. Others tend to specify the size of the animal, i.e. some deal solely with larger animals, some smaller and others only equine. The size of practices varies a great deal. The average size is three or four vets working together and a few are smaller or much larger. Some are incredibly busy, while others may manage to convey an easier atmosphere while being equally hard-working. Some practices offer particular facilities which define them as different types of veterinary practice.

Below is the structure that makes up a general practice.

The structure of a general practice

In a general practice, a veterinary surgeon is responsible for all types of treatment, from medical to surgical, of all animals. It is not uncommon for veterinary surgeons to study for further qualifications offered by the RCVS whilst working in order to further knowledge on certain animals. Veterinary surgeons are vital to the practice and most start as a locum or an associate. Most practices are partnerships run by several veterinary surgeons with one principal. The goal of most associates working in a practice is to reach partnership level. This then involves separate business skills in order to ensure that the practice is making money.

The principal, or practice manager, is usually found in a larger practice as it is important to have one person who has a general overview of the business. This person will be responsible to ensure that all monies are paid and that the practice is run to a high standard. This is not common in all practices as many cannot afford an extra level of support.

From a veterinary surgeon's point of view, the most important people within the practice are veterinary nurses. They ensure that standards of care are high and that both animals and owners are kept comfortable.

They assist in supportive care, and also undertake minor surgical procedures and tests, should they be required, and give the results given to the veterinary surgeons for treatment.

The receptionists are the first point of contact within a practice. A lot of owners will be very disturbed when bringing their animal to the vet and therefore it is their responsibility to present a calm and professional approach that will reassure the clients. They are also gate keepers and personal assistants for the veterinary surgeons, making sure that appointments are managed and times are kept.

Veterinary practice as a small business

The veterinary practice is dependent upon the income it makes that is generated by the surgery itself to be a successful small business. It does not receive money from an external source such as the government. The money that the practice makes is used to pay the staff, the rent (if the site is not owned by the practice) and then the rest is put back into the business to pay for equipment and up to date technology.

Vets are often faced with a moral dilemma when faced with a client who cannot afford to pay the veterinary fees for their services. These can often be very high and many clients (who are used to human healthcare often being free of charge) are shocked by what they are required to pay for treatment for their pets. Vets need to be understanding in this sort of situation but it's important to remember that you are part of a business and this is your livelihood.

Accreditation

All practices need to adhere to the codes of practice of a specific regulatory body.

RCVS Accredited Practice

The RCVS Practice Standards Scheme was launched on 1 January 2005. It is the only scheme representing the veterinary profession and is a regulatory body set up to ensure the highest standards. If you were to work in an RCVS-accredited practice, you would be dedicated to maintaining the highest possible standard of veterinary care; to providing a greater amount of information regarding the care of animals to the public and to clients; and to being at the cutting edge of advancements within the field of veterinary science.

BEVA Listed Practice

The British Equine Veterinary Association (BEVA) has compiled a list of self-certified practices in the equine industry and has a code of practice for veterinary surgeons in this field.

Government service

In the public sector, veterinary surgeons are involved in protecting public health, working in government departments and agencies such as the State Veterinary Service, the Food Standards Agency, the Meat Hygiene Service, the Veterinary Laboratories Agency and the Veterinary Medicines Directorate. Defra employs vets to monitor animal health and to prevent the spread of diseases.

Most of the veterinary surgeons employed by Defra work in the Meat Hygiene Service, the Veterinary Field Service or the Veterinary Investigation Service. Field officers have a wide range of responsibilities which include the control of major epidemic diseases of farm animals, matters of consumer protection (largely in relation to meat hygiene), the control of import and export of animals and the operation of health schemes.

The Veterinary Investigation Service comprises officers who are based in laboratories known as veterinary investigation centres (VICs). Their job is to operate and support control schemes in the interests of public health, to monitor developments and give early warning of any disease problems or dangers to the safety of the food chain. They also provide practising vets with a chargeable diagnostic service. The Central Veterinary Laboratory (CVL) at Weybridge employs veterinary surgeons who carry out research and provide support for various field activities. The Veterinary Medicines Directorate (VMD) deals with the licensing of drugs.

Veterinary teaching and research

Veterinary researchers play a vital role in advancing our understanding of diseases. Research in this field enhances the health, welfare and usefulness of both food-producing and companion animals; and helps to safeguard the public from diseases, many of which were discussed in the previous chapter. Investigations of a comparative nature also help us to understand and manage human disease, for example in cancer, genetics, reproduction and infections. The majority of research takes place at the university veterinary schools and at research institutes (which, unlike veterinary practices, are financed by the government), in laboratories and in private enterprise. Many careers in research span the interface between human and veterinary medicine, which provides a huge scope for variety in the role.

A qualification in veterinary science is more than a licence to practise. It can also open up opportunities for those interested in university teaching and research at home and overseas. In addition to clinical research work, some veterinary surgeons undergo further postgraduate training in the biological sciences. Specialisation is possible in physiology, pathology, microbiology, nutrition, genetics and statistics. Veterinary scientists are not exclusively found working in institutions concerned with animal health and disease; they can also work in natural science laboratories, medical schools and medical research institutes. The opportunities are there for young veterinary surgeons attracted by a research career.

The veterinary schools are among those that provide referral hospitals to which veterinary surgeons can refer cases needing more specialised treatment. For example, recent success in the treatment of equine colic stemmed from early recognition and referral of appropriate cases allied to developments in anaesthesia and monitoring, improved surgical techniques and suture materials, plus better post-operative care. Good teamwork between the referring practitioner and the university specialists plays a big part.

Veterinary graduates are employed as research scientists by Defra, the Biotechnology and Biological Sciences Research Council, the Animal Health Trust, and in pharmaceutical and other industrial research organisations.

New trends

Membership of the EU has brought a new source of income into general practice. This comes about through increased certification required in the interests of safeguarding public health. Every abattoir has to have an official veterinary surgeon to see that it operates hygienically and that slaughtering is humane. Full-time vets are appointed to Defra's Meat Hygiene Service. Every port and airport has to have a veterinary surgeon available. No wonder vets are in short supply.

Other career paths

The Army employs veterinary scientists in the Royal Army Veterinary Corps, where they care for service animals, mostly working dogs and horses used for ceremonial purposes. They also have public health responsibilities and opportunities for research or postgraduate study. Those recruited join in the rank of an Army captain for a four-year Short Service Commission, but this may be altered to a Regular Commission on application.

Table 6 Number and distribution of members of the profession who are economically active

Place of work	2010	2009
General practice	14,843	14,269
Universities	889	811
Research councils	24	24
Industry and commerce	255	221
Charities	479	438
Government	844	804
Total	17,334	16,567

Some veterinary surgeons prefer to work for animal welfare societies, such as the Royal Society for the Prevention of Cruelty to Animals (RSPCA), People's Dispensary for Sick Animals (PDSA) and Blue Cross. Others work as inspectors for the Home Office.

Women in the profession

Over three times as many women are now admitted to veterinary science courses as men (see the table on page 31). They comprise about a third of all the vets in the country, but only one in five of the sole principals in general practice are women. Two explanations have been suggested for this. One is that the statistic reflects past intakes into the profession and this is changing. Another is that whereas women are in the majority at age 30 or younger, they only comprise one in 10 of those aged 50 or over. This suggests that they leave the profession early – perhaps in order to have a family – and do not always return. The figures also hint that they are slightly more inclined than their male colleagues to work in the public sector.

Dealing with people

Being in veterinary practice means that you are running a business. This means that, for example, today's vets have to be familiar with computer records on health and production and know how to interpret them, but there is a more important factor: vets have to be customer-oriented. Students soon pick this up. 'The way we approach people is crucial; it's our bread and butter,' remarked one vet. 'It's the same on the telephone. We make a point of being cheerful and reassuring with a few words of advice until we can get there.' This aspect of practice is now so important that some practices hire a manager to run the administrative side and help to train reception staff. Most courses now make some attempt to introduce the student to the economics of running a practice, although as one vet commented wryly, 'Few will think of book-keeping!'

The professional approach

With increasing professionalism and rising customer expectations come higher overheads. While training, it is vital that a student realises the importance of everything that makes up a surgery. The establishment and maintenance of a modern veterinary surgery now requires a considerable capital sum of money, so most newly qualified vets will start their career by going into practice with other vets. The most ambitious vet will aspire to and attain a partnership after two or three surgery moves; a few will, after gaining experience over three or four years, branch out on their own. Gaining this appreciation is imperative for a vet because it helps to map out their career path: if you can understand what is required by working in practice, you can see what is essential and integral and this will help to shape your approach to your career and perhaps to a future surgery.

Summing up

Many students are interested in becoming veterinary surgeons. For some it will remain a pipe dream either because they lack the ability or skill, or because their ideas about being a veterinary surgeon are not rooted in reality. However, there are real opportunities for those who are motivated and determined to reach their goal. The competition is intense but not impossible and prospective students should be encouraged to explore the veterinary option early by seeking practical experience. As one vet put it, 'See a farm, get your wellies dirty, experience some blood and gore, and see that the life of a vet is not all about cuddly puppies!' This will test both resolve and suitability.

The demand for veterinary services and research-related activities is strong and is increasing. Market forces do dictate the number of places in veterinary schools, but funding limitations imposed by the higher education funding councils are also a controlling factor. Nevertheless, the profession of veterinary surgeon retains its popularity among young people. It is not because of the money, the car, or accommodation – which is often next to the practice ready for instant call-outs. Nor can long hours be the attraction; the provision of a 24-hour service to the public is mandatory. Rather it is probably the sense that being a vet is a way of life rather than a job.

Is being a veterinary surgeon a unique career?

Consider for a moment that the vet has to be a general practitioner with numerous skills and specialisms. Most practitioners are self-employed with wide variations in income, depending upon the type of practice and location. Yet they must make a big capital investment in the latest equipment as veterinary medicine becomes increasingly technical. In the UK there is no state funding for veterinary practice equivalent to the NHS. All the funding comes from the clients (or charities such as the PDSA). Yet vets do not want financial considerations to take over. It is still a caring profession that does not always charge what it should, for example due to compassionate reasons. It is a profession facing immense changes and so it is not surprising that a new career is emerging, that of practice manager. A sensible appointment of a professional manager allows the vets to concentrate on what they do best: dealing with the clients and their animals.

An experienced vet, operating a mixed practice on the Wirral, put the unique qualities of being a vet this way: 'I think people respect what we do. Every Friday a lady brings us a chocolate cake. It's little things like this that make you feel appreciated.' A vet is many things – skilled surgeon, business manager, counsellor and confidant. Vets know that for their clients the animals are often the most important thing in their lives. They have tremendous responsibility for the animals, whether in sickness or in health, and when all other options have failed they have the authority and power vested in them by law to take the animal's life. They devote their lives to animal welfare but it is not based on sentimentality. Find out whether it is the life for you and if it is, go for it.

Table 7 Expected annual earnings

Salary	Region
£26,715	East of England
£45,044	London
£30,500	Northern Ireland
£30,250	North West
£33,500	Scotland
£46,000	Midlands
£32,500	Yorkshire and North East
£35,667	South East
£32,900	South West

Reprinted with kind permission from mysalary.co.uk

Case study

'Are you ever truly prepared for the realities of such a demanding job?' This is a very difficult question to answer. Kim qualified from Edinburgh six years ago and is currently working in general practice. 'You can never underestimate the importance of sound theory and training, but more than that, you can never underestimate the value of experience. I got first-rate training from Edinburgh – the balance between scientific and medical aspects of the course was just right, and the emphasis on the practical side of the profession was invaluable. As a result of the hard work undertaken on the course, I had confidence on graduating that I could handle any likely situation. It is amazing how much more there is to learn upon leaving university, though. It was almost as though the course had merely scratched the surface. This, of course, is not the case, but it is true to say that only by putting the theory into practice can an aspiring vet appreciate what it is like to be a vet.

'It is a job with incredible diversity and indeed diversity that can change on a knife edge. With all the changes in the industry and the current economic and political climate, which does have an effect on the veterinary world as well, it is of the utmost importance that any professional keeps themselves well informed. This can be hard as a vet's hours are long and arduous – but keep your ear to the ground. It is known as continuing professional development (CPD) and it is a requirement of the RCVS. It might seem like the last thing you wish to do after a long week, but CPD allows vets to network with others in the profession through training sessions where we can discuss the updated trends.'

Like many other vets we have heard from, Kim's interest in veterinary science started when she was very young, when she used to go riding with a friend back home in Birmingham. Unlike many others, though, Kim was accepted to veterinary school as a graduate, only arriving at the decision to work in the veterinary profession after first studying for a degree in biology. Having made this decision late, Kim had to take any opportunity in order to gain the relevant work experience, so she appreciates the value of hard work and likes those who undertake work experience with her to display that same drive. Now Kim is working as a veterinary surgeon and hopes to own her own practice in the not-too-distant future.

10| Don't count your chickens before they've hatched
Further information

Do not ever make the mistake of believing that you know enough, because you can always find out more. If you want to be the cat that got the cream, do your research. You will be more likely to get to your number one choice of university if you do your own investigations about where you want to go.

Remember, there is no harm in entering into a dialogue with an admissions tutor if you are asking pertinent and considered questions. An elephant never forgets and neither does an admissions tutor.

Listed below are the contact details of the veterinary schools in the UK and websites of other organisations that might help your research.

Veterinary schools in the UK

BRISTOL
Department of Clinical Veterinary Science
University of Bristol
Langford House
Langford BS40 5DU
Tel (veterinary admissions): 0117 928 8153
Fax (general admissions): 0117 925 1424
Email: vet-ug-admissions@bristol.ac.uk
Website: www.bris.ac.uk

CAMBRIDGE
Veterinary Admission Enquiries Adviser
Department of Veterinary Medicine
University of Cambridge
Madingley Road
Cambridge CB3 0ES
Tel: 01223 330811
Fax: 01223 337610
Email: application.advice@vet.cam.ac.uk
Website: www.vet.cam.ac.uk

EDINBURGH
The Admissions Officer
Royal (Dick) School of Veterinary Studies
University of Edinburgh
Easter Bush Veterinary Centre
Roslin EH25 9RG
Tel: 0131 650 6178
Fax: 0131 650 6585
Website: www.vet.ed.ac.uk

GLASGOW
Admissions Office
Faculty of Veterinary Medicine
University of Glasgow
Bearsden Road
Glasgow G61 1QH
Tel: 0141 330 2225
Fax: 0141 942 7215
Email: admissions@vet.gla.ac.uk
Website: www.gla.ac.uk/faculties/vet

LIVERPOOL
Admissions Sub-Dean
Faculty of Veterinary Science
University of Liverpool
Liverpool L69 7ZJ
Tel: 0151 794 4797
Email: vetadmit@liverpool.ac.uk
Website: www.liv.ac.uk/vets

LONDON
The Registry
Royal Veterinary College
University of London
Royal College Street
London NW1 0TU
Tel: 020 7468 5148
Fax: 020 7388 2342
Email: registry@rvc.ac.uk
Website: www.rvc.ac.uk

NOTTINGHAM
Admissions Team
School of Veterinary Medicine and Science
University of Nottingham
Sutton Bonington Campus
College Road
Sutton Bonington LE12 5RD
Tel: 0115 951 6464

Fax: 0115 951 6415
Email: veterinary-enquiries@nottingham.ac.uk
Website: www.nottingham.ac.uk/vet

Other contacts and sources of information

Useful organisations and websites

- Animal Welfare Foundation: www.bva-awf.org.uk
- Blue Cross: www.bluecross.org.uk
- British Equine Veterinary Association: www.beva.org.uk
- British Veterinary Association: www.bva.co.uk. This is the national representative body for the British veterinary profession.
- Department for Environment, Food and Rural Affairs (Defra): www.defra.gov.uk
- Mander Portman Woodward: www.mpw.co.uk/getintomed
- People's Dispensary for Sick Animals: www.pdsa.org.uk

Royal College of Veterinary Surgeons
Belgravia House
62–64 Horseferry Road
London SW1P 2AF
Tel: 020 7222 2001
Email: education@rcvs.org.uk
Website: www.rcvs.org.uk

St George's University
University Centre
Grenada
West Indies
Tel: 0800 169 9061
Email: sguinfo@sgu.edu
Website: www.sgu.edu

Society of Practising Veterinary Surgeons
www.spvs.org.uk
Provides advice to veterinary surgeons.

Super Vets
www.rvc.ac.uk/supervets
Website for the BBC series about vets at the Royal Veterinary College, London Zoo and Whipsnade Wild Animal Park.

Universities and Colleges Admissions Service: www.ucas.com

Vetsonline
www.vbd.co.uk
Online database and resource.

Courses

VetCam
Tel: 01223 337701
Two-day residential Introduction to Veterinary Science in Cambridge course held in March.

Vetsix
www.workshop-uk.com
Two-day conference organised by the Workshop University Conferences for interested sixth-formers and held annually at Nottingham.

Publications

Student, Finance
www.direct.gov.uk/en/EducationAndLearning

Getting Into Oxford & Cambridge, 2012 entry (publication date April 2011)
Trotman, £12.99.

Guide to Student Money 2011, 16th edition
Trotman, £16.99.

Heap 2012: University Degree Course Offers, 42nd edition (publication date May 2011)
Brian Heap, Trotman, £32.99.

How to Complete Your UCAS Application 2012 Entry, 23rd edition (publication date April 2011)
Trotman, £12.99.
Works through the application procedure step by step using examples, and includes information on how to avoid the most common mistakes and how to write a winning personal statement.

Student Loans – A Guide to Applying
Free, Student Loans Company, 100 Bothwell Street, Glasgow G2 7JD; www.slc.co.uk.